EAT THE WEEK

To the grandparents, for all the
shepherd's pies and lettuce soups

EAT THE WEEK

every meal, every day

ANNA BARNETT

MURDOCH BOOKS

CONTENTS

EATING THE WEEK

I was a fat child. One of my parents' favourite memories is of our first family holiday abroad. We were in a restaurant in Rimini, on Italy's east coast. Not yet a year old, I was full to the brim with spaghetti bolognese, my hands and face smothered with thick red sauce. I hadn't quite mastered cutlery and apparently decided to use the restaurant's floor-to-ceiling curtains, which were made of white lace, to wipe up the bits that hadn't made it into my mouth. Luckily for my parents, the waiters had taken a shine to me and found it amusing. Using soft furnishings instead of napkins is not a habit I've retained in adulthood – although eating spaghetti bolognese definitely is. I suspect my experience all those years ago on the Adriatic Riviera may have set the tone for a lifetime of foodie indulgence and mess.

Another formative influence was my family. I grew up with five siblings: four other girls and one boy. Mealtimes were always around the table, and the TV had to be turned off. If I helped with the cooking, it meant I didn't have to sign up for other chores – and this gave me more eating time. Sundays were all about roast dinners, and Dad would always pile up our plates. While some people are into sweet things, and others are more into savoury, I've always really liked both. Grandma's fluoro lettuce soup, Dad's meatloaf and Nan's upside down cake and mince pies are the things that make me excited. Not just satisfied or happy: excited. As I've got older, I've slightly improved my sense of moderation. But the thrill and excitement remain. And I can still (proudly) put away a decent amount of food if I put my mind to it.

I grew up having to cook in bulk, and carried on doing so when I moved away from home, cooking for housemates, friends, boyfriends, various waifs and strays... pretty much whoever was around. Recently I've been running pop-up restaurants in the converted pub we call home, packing in as many people as possible, up to sixty a night. I rope in friends, family and neighbours to help – they provide furniture, cutlery, serving skills, even entertainment. Every pop-up has a different theme, because I love such a variety of food that I can't choose just one cuisine and stick to it. Pop-ups are the perfect way to indulge your culinary curiosity while challenging your imagination.

This book is drawn from all my enthusiasms and experiences: it's food from and for the lives many of us lead. Its aim is to serve as inspiration for fun, delicious dishes that you can dip in and out of, and that reflect real lives and real lifestyles. We've all had big weekends that have left us gawping in horror at our bank balance come Monday morning. For days like those, you need thrifty but tasty recipes to ease the pressure on your pocket: hence my plans for Budget Mondays. All you need to do is choose whether you fancy Carbs for Comfort or something Wholesome & Healthy. The same goes for the rest of the week: you choose where your head's at (and your stomach), and I'll do my best to provide the answer. Lazy Tuesdays, Cooking for Company Thursdays... all building up to Saturday, which is when I like to do Something Special – whether I'm On a Budget, or blowing the budget entirely by Splashing the Cash.

Hopefully, this book will help guide you and your larder through the week: the healthy, the not-so-healthy, meals cooked post-run or post-pub, prep times from 10 minutes to 10 hours... there are even dishes that will turn your leftovers into brand new meals.

Get stuck in!

BUDGET MONDAYS

These dishes are perfect for when you're feeling slightly guilty after an over-indulgent weekend. You've spent a good wedge of your pay packet, and you're going one of two ways: Wholesome & Healthy or Carbs for Comfort. The former is for those who like to start the week with good intentions, while the latter is for anyone still feeling the repercussions of a hectic or boozy weekend. Equally time- and budget-conscious, they'll help steady you for the week ahead.

BREAKFAST
Scrambled Eggs with Avocado, Chilli Oil & Gherkins (v)
You've woken up with good intentions. The road to healthiness starts here.

LUNCH
Spiced Up Shredded Meat & Sticky Pickled Beetroot Salad
Still on the right track. Keen to keep off the carbs and get the Sunday leftovers used up.

SNACK
Chilli Kale Chips (v)
Keeping the metabolism going... up for a light snack.

WHOLESOME&HEALTHY

DINNER
Nearly Carb Free Fishy Fish Pie
You've managed to make it through Monday... some exercise has happened, so you're in need of something hearty.

DESSERT
Beet 'n' Blueberry Suck Yourself Slim Smoothie (v)
No need to skip dessert.

LEFTOVERS
Fishcakes with Spicy Roasted Tomato Salsa
If you've not scoffed the lot for dinner, use up the leftovers.

(v) = vegetarian option

Preparation time: 5 minutes | **Cooking time:** 10 minutes | **Feeds:** 4

SCRAMBLED EGGS WITH AVOCADO, CHILLI OIL & GHERKINS

This is super-simple, but makes a rounded meal to kick-start the day. I like the contrast between the sweet gherkins and hot chilli oil (I'm in love with the pots of it you get from the Vietnamese supermarket). You'll be well awake once you've scoffed this.

6 organic or free-range eggs

2 tablespoons low-fat crème fraîche (sour cream)

4 slices of pumpernickel bread

2 avocados, sliced

4 large gherkins (pickles), sliced lengthways

1 spring onion (scallion), thinly sliced

squeeze of lime juice

1 tablespoon chilli oil, or more to taste

Whisk the eggs and crème fraîche in a bowl, season with salt and pepper, then transfer to a non-stick frying pan. Cook over medium–low heat, using a spatula (not a whisk) to gently stir the eggs, so you end up with generous soft lumps of egg.

Toast the bread, then plate up, starting with the toast. Place the eggs and avocado on top, followed by the gherkins. Finish with a few slices of spring onion , a squeeze of lime juice and a drizzle of chilli oil, or more if you're up for a bit of heat.

Preparation time: 3 minutes | **Cooking time:** 5 minutes | **Feeds:** 4–6

SPICED UP SHREDDED MEAT &
STICKY PICKLED BEETROOT SALAD

Salads can be pretty dull, but there's no chance of that with this one, which transforms left-over meat into a whole new meal. It's worth trying to save a bowl of pork, lamb or beef from your Sunday roast or barbecue – they all work well. For a bit of extra heat, add more chilli flakes and Tabasco sauce.

350 g (12 oz) cooked pork,
    lamb or beef
dash of olive oil
½ teaspoon chilli flakes
small dash of Tabasco sauce
1 teaspoon runny honey
1 tablespoon black sesame seeds
200 g (7 oz) lamb's lettuce
1 small red Asian shallot, thinly sliced

STICKY PICKLED BEETROOT
450 g (1 lb) drained baby pickled
    beetroot (beets) – about 650 g
    (1 lb 7 oz) before draining
2 tablespoons pomegranate molasses

Take the left-over meat and use two forks to pull the meat apart, shredding it. Add to a hot frying pan with the olive oil, some salt and pepper, chilli flakes and Tabasco and cook on high for a couple of minutes until the meat starts to darken and go crisp. Add the honey, along with the black sesame seeds, and cook for another minute.

Meanwhile, in another pan, warm the beetroot with the pomegranate molasses for 2–3 minutes, then season with a generous sprinkling of black pepper. Add the meat and stir in well.

Arrange a bed of lamb's lettuce and shallot slices on a platter, then stack the shredded meat and sticky beetroot on top. You'll have the perfect combination of sweet and sour: sweet from the honey and sour from the pomegranate molasses.

TIP If you can't find pomegranate molasses, use balsamic glaze or vinegar instead.

Preparation time: 5 minutes | Cooking time: 20 minutes | Feeds: 4–6

CHILLI KALE CHIPS

I love the idea of making your own kale chips – you can chop and change what you put on them, depending what you fancy. Add a spoonful of peanut butter on those slightly less healthy days, or keep them simple and salted. These are the perfect snack to have hanging around the house. I'd choose them over a packet of crisps any day.

400 g (14 oz) purple or green kale –
    about 1 large bag
large glug of olive oil
1 tablespoon runny honey

SWEET CHILLI DRESSING
1 tablespoon runny honey
glug of extra virgin olive oil
dash of Tabasco sauce
½ teaspoon chilli flakes, or more
    if you can take the heat
½ red chilli, thinly sliced

Preheat the oven to 170°C (325°F/gas mark 3) and place a metal rack over a baking tray.

Roughly chop the kale into bite-size pieces and pat dry with paper towel. In a large bowl, combine the olive oil, honey and a good pinch each of salt and pepper until the honey dissolves, then dip each piece of kale in the honeyed oil to coat, shaking off any excess. Lay the dipped kale onto the metal rack (this will allow the heat to circulate all around the kale) and cook in the oven for 10–15 minutes, turning after 5 minutes so the other side gets crisp.

While the kale is cooking, make the dressing. Whisk all the ingredients until thoroughly combined, then season with a pinch each of salt and pepper.

Once your kale is ready, generously drizzle the dressing over it, ensuring all sides are covered. If you want to be super-thorough, toss the dressing through the kale in a large bowl. Taste for seasoning and spice, then serve.

TIP Keep a close eye on these, as they burn easily.

Preparation time: 20 minutes | Cooking time: 40 minutes | Feeds: 4–6

NEARLY CARB FREE FISHY FISH PIE

This recipe is a great way to eat healthily and still feel like you're having a treat. Admittedly a cheesy mashed potato topping is an obvious winning combination, but this comes close – packed full of flavour and with amazing textures, and the upshot is there'll be no carb coma afterwards.

2 heads of broccoli

1 large cauliflower

glug of rapeseed oil

1 white onion, finely diced

2 garlic cloves, thinly sliced

3 whole star anise

1 large bulb of fennel, roughly diced

1 large leek, sliced into 1 cm (½ in) loops

2 tablespoons plain (all-purpose) flour

200 ml (7 fl oz) white wine – optional

500 ml (17 fl oz/2 cups) fish stock

300 g (10½ oz) sustainable smoked haddock, pin-boned and skinned (ask your fishmonger to do this), then chopped into generous chunks

280 g (10 oz/2 cups) frozen peas

handful of finely chopped parsley

60 g (2¼ oz/⅔ cup) finely grated mature cheddar – leave this out if you're aiming to be a bit healthier

Preheat the oven to 180°C (350°F/gas mark 4).

Cut the broccoli and cauliflower into small florets of roughly the same size. Put in a roasting tin, drizzle with rapeseed oil and season with salt and pepper. Roast for 10–12 minutes until they start to crisp up.

Meanwhile, put the onion, garlic, star anise, fennel and leek in a pan with a glug of oil. Season with salt and pepper, then cook for 3–4 minutes over medium heat until the onion is translucent. Stir in the flour, then add the white wine, if you're using it, and let it bubble for 3 minutes (to cook off the alcohol). Add the fish stock and simmer for 5 minutes, stirring constantly, until the sauce begins to thicken. Add the fish, peas and parsley, then take the pan off the heat, cover and let the fish cook in the hot sauce for 5–6 minutes.

Drain the sauce from the pan and put to one side – you should have about 125 ml (4 fl oz/½ cup). Tip the rest of the contents of the pan into a pie dish, and arrange the cauliflower and broccoli evenly on top. Pour a little sauce over the cauliflower and broccoli, followed by the grated cheese. Brown in the oven for 10 minutes or until golden and bubbling. Serve with the remaining sauce as 'gravy' on the side.

TIP To keep the budget down on this dish, opt for bigger portions of veg over fish, as I've done above. For those more indulgent days, add king prawns, cod cheeks or salmon... anything you can get your hands on.

BEET 'N' BLUEBERRY SUCK YOURSELF SLIM SMOOTHIE

This doubles up as the perfect start or end to any healthy day. I always feel good after this sort of fresh and light smoothie.

1 cooked beetroot (beet) – you can often pick these up ready-cooked in vacuum packs
155 g (5½ oz/1 cup) frozen blueberries
handful of spinach leaves
½ orange, peeled
5 ice cubes

Combine all the ingredients in a blender and blend until smooth. Drink straightaway.

TIP I've opted for ice cubes to add a bit of texture, however almond milk or yogurt work well too.

Preparation time: 20 minutes | Cooking time: 40 minutes | Feeds: 4–6

FISHCAKES WITH SPICY ROASTED TOMATO SALSA

The smoked mackerel adds extra fishiness to these fishcakes, and the spicy tomato salsa really makes them pop!

400 g (14 oz) floury potatoes, such as maris piper, king edward or desiree, peeled and cut into 5 cm (2 in) chunks

½ white onion, finely diced

rapeseed oil for frying

300 g (10½ oz) left-over fish pie (see page 19) or sustainable smoked haddock, pin-boned and skinned

1 bay leaf – if using smoked haddock

150 ml (5 fl oz) milk – if using smoked haddock

100 g (3½ oz) smoked mackerel, broken into generous chunks

2 tablespoons capers, roughly chopped

handful of freshly chopped parsley

2 teaspoons dijon mustard

finely grated zest of ½ lemon

1 egg, lightly beaten

175 g (6 oz/3 cups) breadcrumbs

spicy roasted tomato salsa (see opposite), to serve

2 lemons, cut into quarters

Start by boiling the potatoes in salted water for around 10 minutes or until tender. Lightly fry the onion in a dash of oil for a minute or two until translucent, then put to one side.

If using smoked haddock rather than left-over fish pie, put the fish in a pan with the bay leaf and the milk. Cover and bring to the boil, then lower the heat and simmer for 3 minutes. Take off the heat and let the fish cook in the milk for another 2–3 minutes – it's done when it flakes easily. Remove the fish and set aside.

Drain the potatoes and return to the pan to steam dry. Mash the potatoes, then add the cooked onion, left-over fish pie or haddock, smoked mackerel, capers, parsley, mustard, lemon zest, egg and 60 g (2¼ oz/1 cup) of the breadcrumbs. Season with salt and pepper and combine everything thoroughly.

Spread out the rest of the breadcrumbs on a large plate. Mould a handful of the fishcake mixture into a ball, then flatten slightly and roll in the breadcrumbs to coat. Ideally, leave the fishcakes to chill and set in the fridge for an hour (or all day, if that's easier for you).

When you're ready, cook the fishcakes in a hot frying pan with a generous glug of oil, for around 4–5 minutes on each side. Don't be tempted to turn them too early, or they might break. If your pan isn't large enough to cook them all at once, keep the cooked fishcakes warm in a 150°C (300°F/ gas mark 2) oven.

Smother the fishcakes with the salsa, add a lemon quarter on the side and eat!

SPICY ROASTED TOMATO SALSA

400 g (14 oz) ripe, deep-red tomatoes,
   roughly chopped
glug of rapeseed oil
1 white onion, finely diced
2 cloves garlic, finely diced
1 red chilli, finely diced – remove
   the seeds for a milder salsa
1 tablespoon finely chopped
   pickled jalapeños
handful of chopped coriander (cilantro)
glug of red wine vinegar
juice of 1 lime
dash of Tabasco sauce, to taste
sprinkle of chilli flakes, to taste

Preheat the oven to 190°C (375°F/gas mark 5). Put
the tomatoes in a baking dish with the rapeseed
oil and sprinkle with salt and pepper. Roast for
12–15 minutes or until they soften, then blitz with
a hand blender until smooth and leave to cool.
Combine the remaining ingredients in a bowl,
then add the tomatoes and check the seasoning.

BREAKFAST
Cheesy Bean Ciabatta To Go (v)
Feeling fragile or just tired after the weekend?

LUNCH
Halloumi & Chorizo Salad Wrap
with Gherkin Mustard Mayo
Ready for your second generous feed of the day?

SNACK
Home Baked Vegetable Crisps (v)
You've reached that 4 o'clock lull and are in need of a pick-me-up.

CARBSFORCOMFORT

DINNER
Chilli Guac Mac 'n' Cheese (v)
You've made it through the day; no run in sight, just more food.

DESSERT
Nan's Classic Upside Down Pineapple Cake (v)
Room for one last treat.

LEFTOVERS
Big Boy's Fried Chilli Mac Burger (v)

(v) = vegetarian option

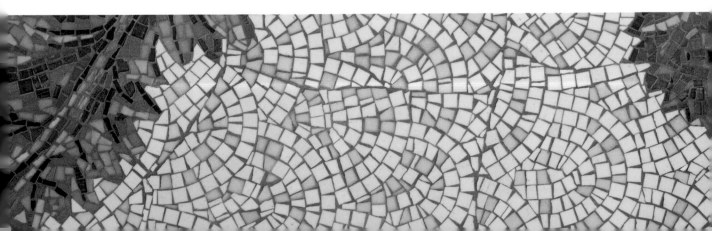

Preparation time: 3 minutes | **Cooking time:** 10 minutes | **Feeds:** 4–6

CHEESY BEAN CIABATTA TO GO

This is pretty much cheesy beans in a ciabatta – there's always gonna be a day that's right for. It's super-simple and tastes so good. Perfect if you're short of time but in need of something stodgy and filling.

2 bake-at-home ciabattas
   or other bread rolls
1 x 400 g (14 oz) tin of baked beans
   in tomato sauce
good glug of Worcestershire sauce
sprinkle of chilli flakes
100 g (3½ oz/⅔ cup) crumbled feta
200 g (7 oz/2 cups) grated mature
   cheddar

Preheat the oven to 180°C (350°F/gas mark 4).

Take the ciabattas and make a small lengthways cut along the middle, being careful not to cut right through. The aim is to try and make as small a hole as possible, to try and keep all the melted cheese and runny beans in while they're cooking.

Mix the beans with the Worcestershire sauce, chilli flakes and some salt and pepper, stirring thoroughly.

Distribute the feta and cheddar evenly between the ciabattas, stuffing the cheese in and spreading it out as best you can. Do the same with the baked beans, then transfer the cheesy bean ciabattas to a baking tray and bake for 7–10 minutes or until golden.

TIP You can wrap these individually in foil to help keep the contents in the ciabatta.

Preparation time: 10 minutes | **Cooking time:** 10 minutes | **Feeds:** 4

HALLOUMI & CHORIZO SALAD WRAP
WITH GHERKIN MUSTARD MAYO

The combination of chorizo and halloumi with crisp raw veg does it for me. This is full of flavour and near on impossible to get wrong. Use up whatever salad you have in the fridge, but make sure you include the fresh herbs – the mint alongside the saltiness of the chorizo and halloumi really works.

250 g (9 oz) chorizo – get the good stuff you slice yourself

250 g (9 oz) halloumi, cut into eight slices and then each slice cut in half

4 soft flour tortillas

200 g (7 oz) gherkins (pickles), finely chopped

1 generous tablespoon American-style mustard

2–3 tablespoons mayonnaise

2 large carrots, grated

¼ red cabbage, finely shredded

handful of finely chopped coriander (cilantro)

handful of mint leaves

Preheat the oven to 160°C (315°F/gas mark 2–3).

Chop the chorizo into rough chunks, then add to a non-stick frying pan and cook over medium heat for a few minutes or until the oil seeps out of the chorizo and the chorizo is slightly crispy. At which point you're ready to add the halloumi – you want to cook it in this richly flavoured oil. Leave to cook over high for a further 3–4 minutes: by not turning the chorizo or halloumi, you'll be left with one side crispy and one side soft, which is perfect for this dish.

Meanwhile, wrap your tortillas in foil and warm through in the oven for 5 minutes.

In a small bowl, combine the gherkins with the mustard, mayonnaise and some pepper. Have the other ingredients (carrot, red cabbage, chopped coriander and mint leaves) ready to assemble your wraps. Start by spreading a spoonful of the mayonnaise along the length of the tortilla, then add the hot chorizo and halloumi, followed by the carrot, red cabbage and herbs. Roll up and serve.

This is also a nice dish to serve up on a platter and let people roll their own. Alternatively, serve as a stack – you can make it look mega by piling up the salad in the middle of the tortilla and adding the chorizo, halloumi and herbs last.

TIP Don't add any extra salt, as both the chorizo and halloumi are already pretty salty.

Preparation time: 10 minutes | **Cooking time:** 20 minutes | **Feeds:** 4

HOME BAKED VEGETABLE CRISPS

Get on board the craze for an alternative to a regular packet of crisps. There's a little less guilt and a lot more enjoyment doing it this way.

2 parsnips
2 beetroot (beets)
1 sweet potato
glug of olive oil

Preheat the oven to 200°C (400°F/gas mark 6). Using a mandoline or food processor, thinly slice all the vegetables, then pat dry with paper towel to remove any excess moisture.

Put the vegetables slices in a large bowl, drizzle very lightly with olive oil and mix to coat. Spread the vegetable slices out on lined baking trays in a single layer and bake for 15–20 minutes, turning them halfway through. Keep an eye on them: it can be hard to tell when the beetroot is ready, but when the parsnip and sweet potato are golden, they'll all be done.

Drain the crisps on paper towel, then sprinkle with salt flakes and pepper.

TIP You'll need a few baking trays for this one, so you can spread out the vegetable slices to get them all crispy.

Preparation time: 15 minutes | **Cooking time:** 30 minutes | **Feeds:** 4–6 (or 2 with leftovers)

CHILLI GUAC MAC 'N' CHEESE

Is there anything more indulgent than a big bowl of mac 'n' cheese? Add the jalapeños and coriander and taste the difference; add the chilli guac topping and really taste the difference! This is a definite crowd-pleaser, so on those days when you're happy to share, make up a big batch – people will love you for it. Enjoy this carb-heavy pot of heaven.

400 g (14 oz) macaroni
120 g (4¼ oz) butter
50 g (1¾ oz/⅓ cup) plain (all-purpose) flour
2 rounded teaspoons dijon mustard
2 bay leaves
1.25 litres (44 fl oz/5 cups) semi-skimmed milk
150 g (5½ oz) pickled jalapeños
4 spring onions (scallions), thinly sliced
handful of finely chopped coriander (cilantro)
250 g (9 oz/2 ½ cups) grated mature cheddar
150 g (5½ oz/1½ cups) finely grated parmesan

CHILLI GUAC TOPPING
2 hass avocados, mashed
200 g (7 oz) pickled jalapeños, finely chopped
2 cloves garlic, finely chopped
juice of 2 limes
small handful of chopped coriander (cilantro)

Start by boiling a large pan of salted water. Add the macaroni and stir thoroughly to ensure the pasta doesn't stick. Continue to do this every few minutes while the pasta cooks. Cook as per the instructions on the packet until the pasta is al dente (still has a slight crunch to it), around 8–12 minutes.

Melt the butter in a large saucepan over medium–low heat. Add the flour and stir until it forms a paste, then add the mustard and bay leaves and season generously with salt and pepper. Gradually add the milk, stirring constantly, until you have a thick creamy sauce. At this point, add the jalapeños, spring onions and coriander, plus half of the grated cheddar and a quarter of the parmesan, saving the rest of the cheeses for the top of the mac 'n' cheese.

Once the cheese has melted and the sauce is smooth, stir in the drained macaroni, then transfer to individual heatproof dishes, or one large one, and cover with the remaining cheeses and some more pepper. Brown under a hot grill (broiler) for 5–7 minutes or until golden and crisp.

For the chilli guac topping, simply combine all the ingredients and season with salt and white pepper. Add a large dollop to every serving.

Preparation time: 10 minutes | **Cooking time:** 35 minutes | **Feeds:** 6–8 (or 2, if you're sharing with me)

NAN'S CLASSIC UPSIDE DOWN PINEAPPLE CAKE

My nan has made this cake 'for donkey's years', as she would say. And the best bit is she's still making it. Nan knows what she's doing when it comes to baking – she's a pro.

120 g (4¼ oz) butter, at room
    temperature
120 g (4¼ oz) caster (superfine) sugar
2 eggs
180 g (6¼ oz) self-raising
    (self-rising) flour
2 tablespoons milk
cream or vanilla ice cream, to serve

PINEAPPLE TOPPING
60 g (2¼ oz) butter, at room
    temperature
60 g (2¼ oz) brown sugar
8 tinned pineapple rings
8 glacé cherries

Preheat the oven to 180°C (350°F/gas mark 4) and line the base of a 23–25 cm (9–10 in) non-stick cake tin with baking paper.

For the pineapple topping, beat together the butter and brown sugar until creamy, then spread over the base of the tin. Lay the pineapple rings on top in a single layer and place a cherry in the centre of each ring.

Cream the butter and sugar until pale and fluffy, then add the eggs one at a time. Sift in the flour and beat thoroughly, then stir in the milk and keep mixing until you have a smooth batter. Pour into the tin and cook in a moderate oven (as Nan would put it) – that is, bake on the middle shelf of your preheated oven for 30–35 minutes. Cool for a minute or two, then turn out onto a plate.

Nan suggests serving with cream or ice cream... sometimes both is a good option, and if my grandad's got anything to do with it, he'll definitely encourage that.

TIP Tinned apricots or peaches make a great topping for this cake too, but why mess with a winning formula?

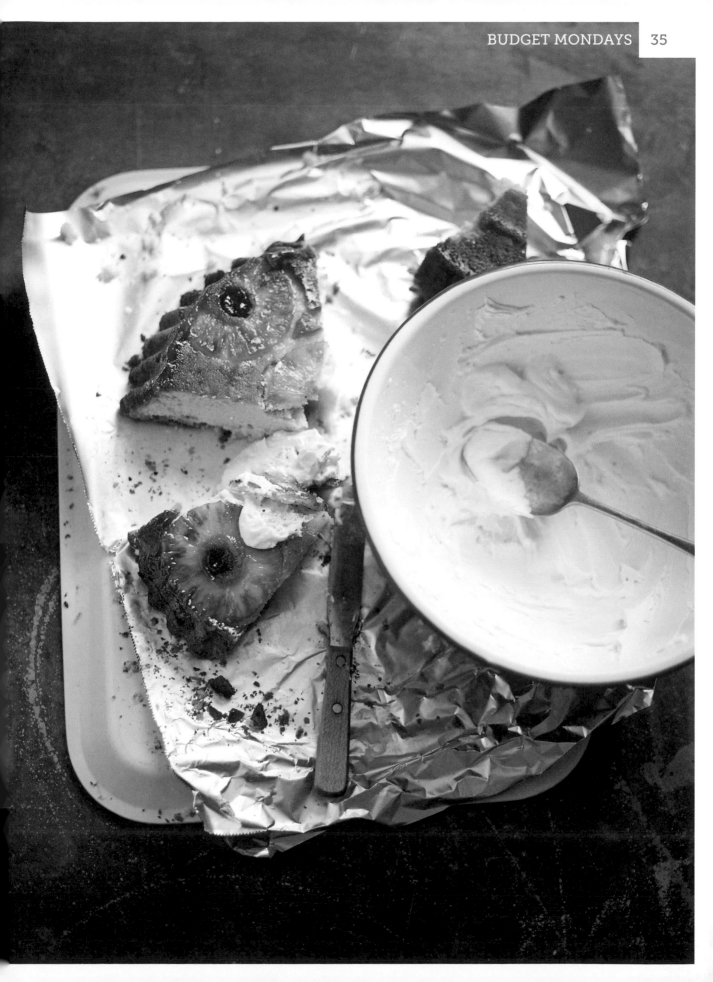

Preparation time: 3 minutes | Cooking time: 10 minutes | Feeds: 4

BIG BOY'S FRIED CHILLI MAC BURGER

This is ideal for any vegetarian feeling bereft without a burger. I'm 100% certain this is the food my vegetarian boyfriend regularly dreams about. It really is that good. I'd actually go as far as to say it's worth making the mac 'n' cheese just so you can make these 'burgers' with the leftovers. Note to self: this is not for a diet day... and should be eaten during an exercise-heavy week!

4 processed cheese slices – trust me, these are the best for this

4 good-quality burger buns

2 large gherkins (pickles), thinly sliced into strips

4 slices beef (beefsteak) tomato

1 hass avocado, sliced (or use left-over chilli guac; see page 33)

BURGERS

4 large spoonfuls of left-over mac 'n' cheese (see page 33)

rapeseed oil for frying

BURGER SAUCE

4 tablespoons mayonnaise

2 tablespoons ketchup (tomato sauce)

1 tablespoon American-style mustard

1 tablespoon red wine vinegar

1½ teaspoons chipotle Tabasco sauce

1 large gherkin (pickle), finely diced

Fairly portion up the left-over mac 'n' cheese, being as generous as you can – no one's going to want the small portion here. Heat a generous glug of rapeseed oil in a large frying pan over high heat and cook the mac 'n' cheese 'burgers' for 3–4 minutes on each side or until golden and crisp. When they are cooked on one side, carefully turn them over and place a cheese slice on top of each one. Cook until the other side is well browned and crispy and the cheese has melted.

For the burger sauce, combine all the ingredients and season with salt and pepper. Adjust the level of spice to your taste by adding more Tabasco for extra heat, or more mayo and ketchup for less heat.

Slice the burger buns in half and spoon a generous coating of burger sauce onto both halves. Place some strips of gherkin, a slice of tomato and a couple of slices of avocado on the bottom half of each bun, then season.

Once the 'burgers' are cooked to crisp and golden perfection and the cheese slice has melted over the top, place them on the buns, cover with the top half of the bun and get stuck in.

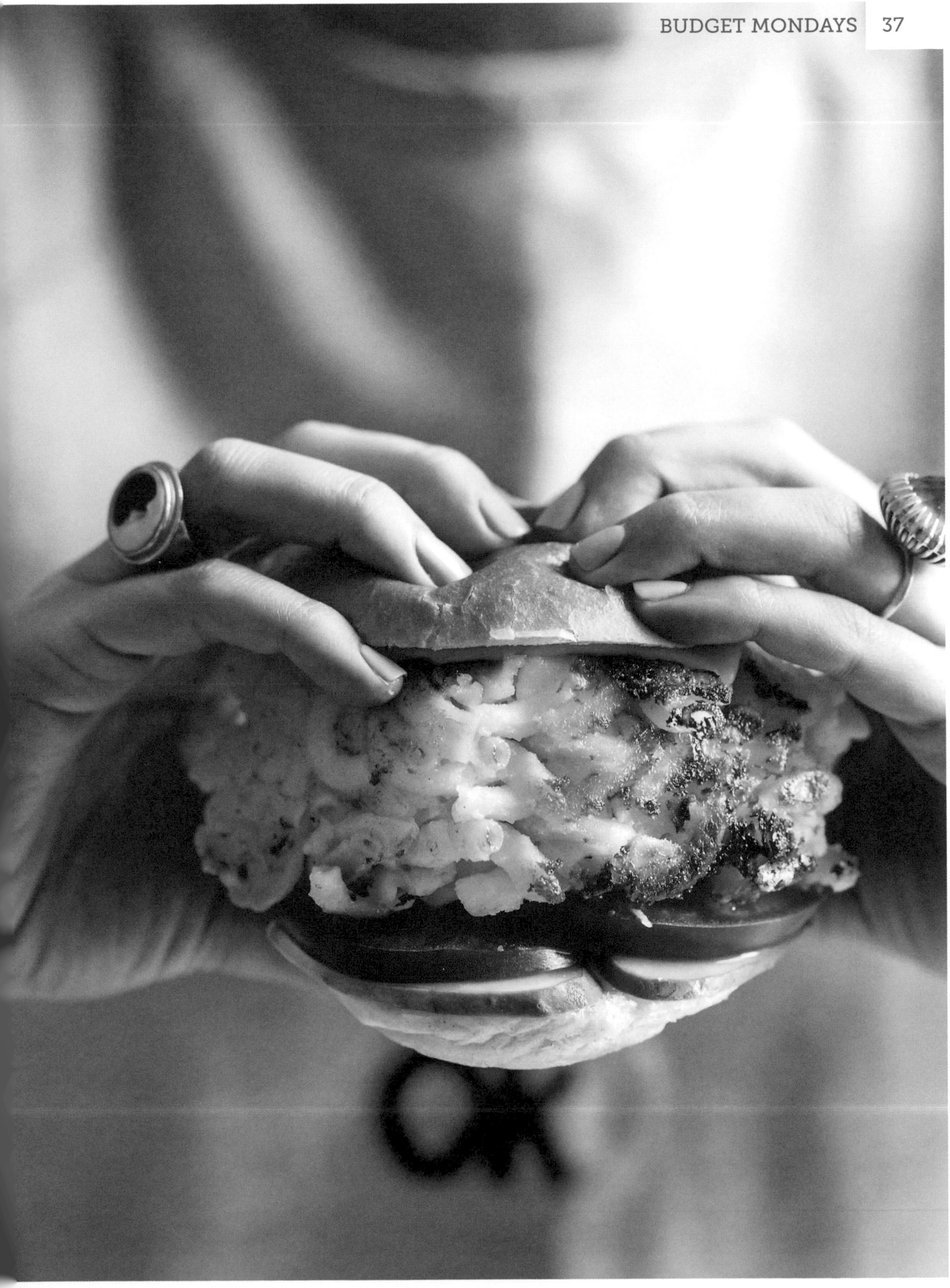

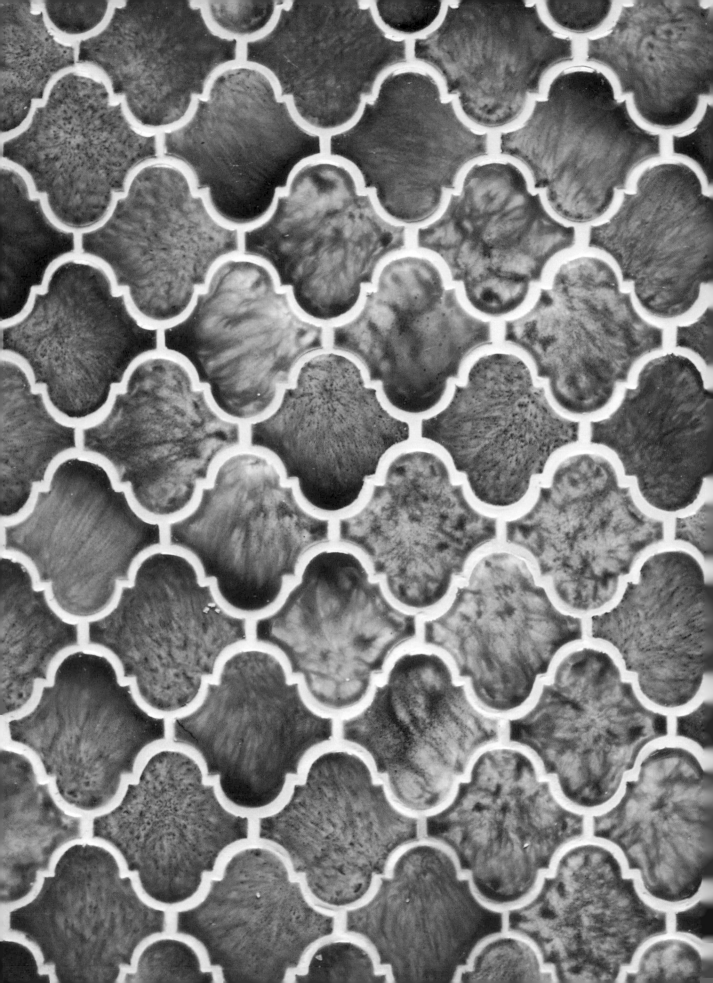

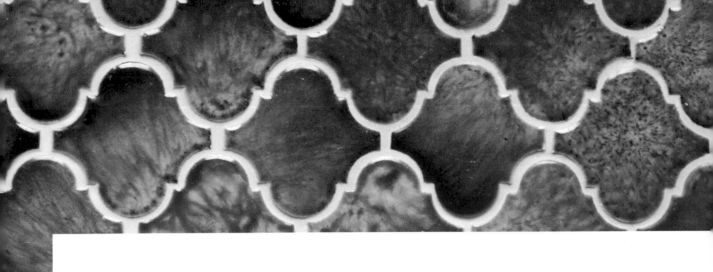

LAZY TUESDAYS

Dinner parties, dates, meals out or big plans don't happen on a Tuesday. By Tuesday we're still belly-deep in the working week, and most of us want to stay on the straight and narrow just a little longer. That said, Tuesdays are also pretty much always *lazy*, and Tuesday's dishes should require minimum effort, helping conserve your energy for the rest of the week to come. I've included a Cornershop Dash option for when ingredients are hard to come by, and a Supermarket Run for those willing to go further or who have already stocked up for the week. Whatever route you take, think 'one pot and you're done' – less time cooking and less time washing up.

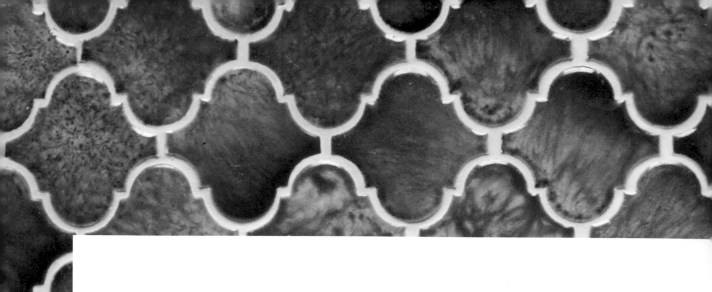

BREAKFAST
Crunchy Oat Bocker Glory Breakfast (v)
Working with what the cornershop and cupboards have to offer.

LUNCH
Grandma Rita's Legendary Lettuce Soup (v)
After a healthy start, you're carrying on the theme – minimum effort needed here.

SNACK
Mega Triple Decker Triple Cheese Toastie (v)
Feeling good after a light lunch, but in need of a treat.

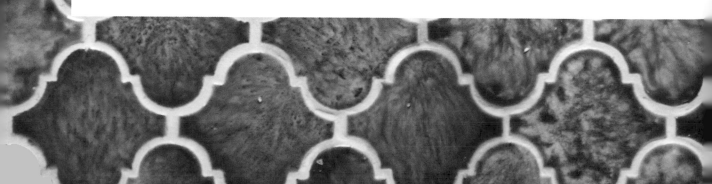

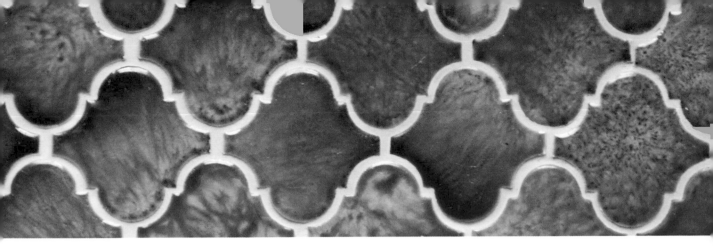

CORNERSHOPDASH

DINNER
All The Good Stuff Shakshuka Style with
Dippy Eggs & Garlic Croutons (v)
Post large snack, you're keeping dinner light.

DESSERT
Lemon Yogurt Pancakes with Lemon Drizzle (v)
Room for a little extra?

LEFTOVERS
Bean & Tomato Stew with Melted Feta
& Roasted Shallots (v)

(v) = vegetarian option

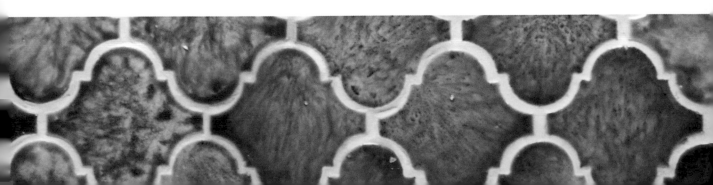

Preparation time: 5 minutes | **Feeds:** 1

CRUNCHY OAT BOCKER GLORY BREAKFAST

This is a beautiful breakfast dish that takes no time at all. You'll definitely be starting the day on the right foot after this.

150 g (5½ oz) thick Greek-style yogurt
125 g (4½ oz/1 cup) granola
4 dried apricots
1 teaspoon honey
4 large strawberries (or any fruit that's in season), chopped

Place a dollop of yogurt in a dessert glass, followed by a third of the granola, then another dollop of yogurt, followed by the apricots and a drizzle of honey. Add another third of the oats, then the rest of the yogurt. Finish with the rest of the oats, the strawberries and a final drizzle of honey.

TIP Opt for low-fat live yogurt for a healthier option, or try frozen yogurt for a refreshing start to the day. And don't be afraid to mix it up by using other kinds of fruit.

Preparation time: 10 minutes | **Cooking time:** 20 minutes | **Feeds:** 4–6

GRANDMA RITA'S LEGENDARY LETTUCE SOUP

Don't turn the page on this one. It may not sound like it'll be the best thing you've ever eaten – but believe me, this is so good. It's one of the things I most remember eating from my childhood. Grandma would make this time and time again for us, and I could never get enough of it...

1 large white onion, roughly chopped
large knob of butter
2 bibb (butter) lettuces, roughly
   shredded
1 litre (35 fl oz/4 cups) vegetable stock
500 ml (17 fl oz/2 cups) milk
1 romaine (cos) lettuce, roughly
   shredded
crème fraîche (sour cream) and
   rocket (arugula), to serve

Take a large saucepan and add the onion, along with the butter. Season with salt and pepper and cook over medium–low heat for a few minutes until the onion softens.

Add the bibb lettuce, vegetable stock and milk, then bring to the boil and cook for around 10 minutes until the lettuce wilts.

Remove from the heat and add the romaine lettuce, stir and allow to cool for a few minutes before blending until smooth. Check for seasoning – I love a little extra white pepper here.

Return the soup to the pan and gently reheat. Ladle into bowls, add a dollop of crème fraîche and a handful of rocket, then serve.

Preparation time: 5 minutes | **Cooking time:** 5 minutes | **Feeds:** 1–2

MEGA TRIPLE DECKER
TRIPLE CHEESE TOASTIE

The triple decker bit is optional here – a regular cheese toastie is just as delicious. However, there are definitely days when three slices are needed.

3 x 1 cm (½ in) thick slices
   of wholegrain bread
2 tablespoons crème fraîche
   (sour cream)
120 g (4¼ oz/¾ cup) finely
   crumbled feta
125 g (4½ oz/1¼ cups) finely grated
   parmesan
125 g (4½ oz/1¼ cups) grated
   mature cheddar
1 spring onion (scallion), finely
   shredded into long strips
big knob of butter
glug of olive oil

Spread a slice of bread with half the crème fraîche, then top with half of all the cheeses, followed by the spring onion. Season with salt and pepper, then place another slice of bread on top and press down firmly, so you won't lose too much cheese out the sides when you're cooking your toastie. Spread the remainder of the crème fraîche over this slice of bread, then sprinkle over the rest of the cheeses, and finish with the last slice of bread, again pressing down firmly.

Heat the butter and oil in a frying pan for a moment or two, then cook your toastie over medium–high heat for 2–3 minutes on each side, or until the cheese has started to melt and the bread is crisp and golden. Serve straightaway.

Preparation time: 10 minutes | Cooking time: 25 minutes | Feeds: 4–6 (or 2 with leftovers)

ALL THE GOOD STUFF SHAKSHUKA STYLE WITH DIPPY EGGS & GARLIC CROUTONS

I love this dish. It's simple and hard to get wrong, which means it's perfect as a brunch, lunch or dinner dish. The spices, combined with runny-yolked eggs, feta and fresh herbs work a treat. This is also great as a sharing dish, so don't save it just for lazy Tuesdays.

glug of olive oil

1 red onion, roughly chopped

3 cloves garlic, crushed and
   roughly chopped

1 red chilli, thinly sliced

small handful of oregano leaves,
   thinly sliced

2 teaspoons smoked paprika

2 teaspoons ground cumin

2 x 400 g (14 oz) tins of cherry tomatoes

4–6 free-range eggs –one per person

150 g (5½ oz) feta, crumbled

handful of roughly chopped coriander
   (cilantro)

handful of roughly chopped parsley

GARLIC CROUTONS

1 fresh crusty loaf

glug of olive oil

2 cloves garlic, cut in half lengthways

small handful of roughly chopped
   parsley

Start by pouring a glug of oil into a skillet or frying pan over medium heat, then add the onion, garlic, chilli, oregano, paprika and cumin. Season with salt and pepper and cook, stirring occasionally, for a few minutes until the onion softens, then add the tinned cherry tomatoes. Once the sauce starts to bubble, lower the heat and simmer for 10–15 minutes to let the flavours deepen.

Crack in the eggs, spacing them out evenly. Turn the heat up to high, cover the pan with a lid or foil and cook for 3–4 minutes or until the egg whites are set but the yolks are still runny.

While the shakshuka cooks, chop or tear your loaf into roughly 2.5–5 cm (1–2 in) hunks. Heat a frying pan over medium–high heat and add a glug of oil, followed by the bread. Fry the croutons until golden brown all over, shaking the pan every now and then. When you're happy with the level of crunch, drain the croutons on paper towel, then rub all over with the cut side of the garlic cloves and sprinkle with parsley.

Serve the shakshuka topped with a generous sprinkle of feta, coriander and parsley and a grinding of black pepper. Scatter over the garlic croutons, then place in the middle of the table and let people help themselves.

Preparation time: 5 minutes | **Cooking time:** 15 minutes | **Feeds:** 4

LEMON YOGURT PANCAKES WITH LEMON DRIZZLE

When you need a treat, you can whip this up with minimum effort – and get someone else to do the frying! This batter is light, fluffy and zesty.

150 g (5½ oz/1 cup) plain
   (all-purpose) flour
½ teaspoon baking powder
½ teaspoon bicarbonate of soda
   (baking soda)
1 tablespoon caster (superfine) sugar
190 g (6¾ oz/⅔ cup) Greek-style
   yogurt
80 ml (2½ fl oz/⅓ cup) semi-
   skimmed milk
2 tablespoons lemon juice
finely grated zest of 1 lemon
knob of butter, melted and left to cool
glug of rapeseed oil
mint leaves, to serve

LEMON DRIZZLE

2 tablespoons brown sugar,
   or more to taste
juice of 2 lemons
finely grated zest of 1 lemon

Combine the flour, baking powder, bicarbonate of soda, sugar and a pinch of salt in a large bowl. In a separate bowl, whisk together the yogurt, milk, lemon juice and zest and butter. Pour into the large bowl and combine to make a thick batter.

Pour a small glug of rapeseed oil into a non-stick frying pan over medium heat. Working in batches, cook small ladlefuls of the batter, frying the pancakes for around 2–3 minutes on each side or until golden. Repeat until all the batter has been used up.

For the lemon drizzle, combine the sugar, lemon juice and zest with a splash of water in a small saucepan. Warm over low heat until the sugar dissolves – this should only take a few minutes.

Stack the pancakes on plates and pour over the lemon drizzle. Top with sprigs of mint and serve.

TIP Keep the cooked pancakes warm in a 150°C (300°F/gas mark 2) oven while you cook the rest.

Preparation time: 10 minutes | **Cooking time:** 25 minutes | **Feeds:** 4–6

BEAN & TOMATO STEW
WITH MELTED FETA &
ROASTED SHALLOTS

This dish always surprises me as it's so simple but tastes so good... even better when you're using up left-over shakshuka. The sweet, sticky roasted shallots are a brilliant addition.

glug of rapeseed oil

1 red onion, roughly chopped

1 carrot, roughly diced

3 cloves garlic, roughly chopped

2 x 400 g (14 oz) tins of chickpeas, drained

1 x 400 g (14 oz) tin of butter beans, drained

1 x 400 g (14 oz) tin of tomatoes

2 large ladlefuls of left-over shakshuka (see page 49)

1 teaspoon ground cumin

1 teaspoon dried oregano

250 g (9 oz) feta, broken into large chunks

handful of roughly chopped parsley

ROASTED SHALLOTS

4 banana shallots, peeled and cut in half lengthways

few sprigs of thyme

generous glug of rapeseed oil

For the roasted shallots, preheat the oven to 190°C (375°F/gas mark 5). Place the shallots and thyme in a roasting tin, drizzle with rapeseed oil and season with salt and pepper. Roast for 15–20 minutes or until golden and sticky.

Meanwhile, for the bean and tomato stew, pour a glug of rapeseed oil into a large pan over medium–high heat, then add the onion and carrot and cook until they start to soften. Add the garlic, cook for a minute, then tip in the chickpeas, butter beans, tomatoes and left-over shakshuka. Season with the cumin, oregano, salt and pepper and cook for 10–15 minutes or until everything is hot and bubbling. About 5 minutes before serving, add the chunks of feta and a generous garnish of chopped parsley. Serve the roasted shallots alongside.

TIP If you got carried away with the shakshuka at dinner and don't have much (or any) left over, just add another tin of tomatoes and a teaspoon of smoked paprika instead.

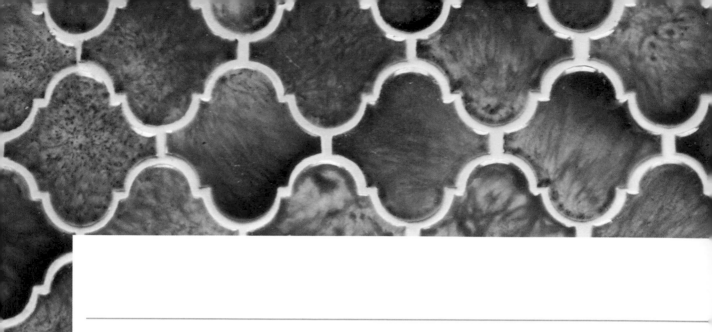

BREAKFAST
Oeufs Cocotte with Prosciutto &
Crusty Breadcrumb Topping
*Tuesdays are tricky. There's almost a whole week ahead of you...
time for a hearty start.*

LUNCH
All the Greens Super Crunchy Salad (v)
Get in there early and tick off your five a day.

SNACK
Basil Butter Corn (v)
Still in the mood for something fresh?

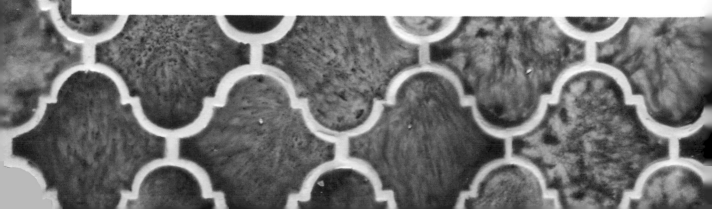

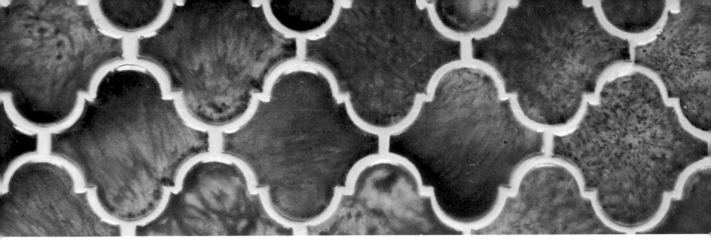

SUPERMARKETRUN

DINNER
Sweet Pork & Date Ragout
In need of something simple but big on flavour?

DESSERT
Pear & Stem Ginger Tarte Tatin
with Cardamom Cream (v)
Craving something sweet?

LEFTOVERS
Sticky Pork and Pineapple Pad Thai

(v) = vegetarian option

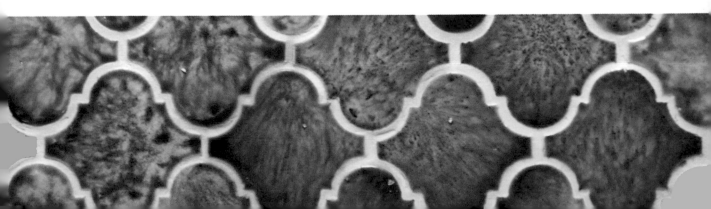

OEUFS COCOTTE
WITH PROSCIUTTO & CRUSTY BREADCRUMB TOPPING

This is a delicious dish packed with flavour. You'll impress yourself with this one – it looks and tastes amazing.

4 slices of prosciutto
150 g (5½ oz) crème fraîche
   (sour cream)
4 free-range eggs
4 cherry tomatoes, cut into quarters
1 spring onion (scallion), thinly sliced

BREADCRUMBS
2 slices of bread, ideally a bit stale
25 g (1 oz/¼ cup) finely grated
   parmesan
small handful of finely chopped
   parsley

Preheat the oven to 190°C (375°F/gas mark 5).

Take four small ovenproof serving dishes and lay a slice of prosciutto in the base of each one, followed by a dollop of crème fraîche. Season with salt and pepper, then crack an egg into each dish, followed by another dollop of crème fraîche and the cherry tomatoes.

Blitz the bread in a blender or finely chop with a sharp knife to make breadcrumbs. Combine with the parmesan and parsley, then season with black pepper and sprinkle over each dish.

Bake for 6–7 minutes or until the breadcrumb crust is golden and the egg whites are set but the yolks are still runny. If the eggs are cooked before the breadcrumbs brown, blast them under a hot grill (broiler) for a minute or two – just keep an eye on them so they don't burn. Garnish with spring onion and a sprinkle of pepper and serve.

Preparation time: 10 minutes | **Cooking time:** 20 minutes | **Feeds:** 4–6

ALL THE GREENS SUPER CRUNCHY SALAD

I'm a huge fan of salads... as long as they're good ones. Feel free to swap ingredients in or out here – the main thing is to get plenty of variety and different textures together in one bowl. This can be easily adapted for lunch at the office: if you remember, blanch the broccoli and roast the spring onions the night before; otherwise, just eat them raw.

200 g (7 oz) spring onions (scallions)
glug of rapeseed oil
250 g (9 oz) broccoli, cut into
   small florets
½ head of purple or white cauliflower,
   cut into small florets
200 g (7 oz) purple sprouting broccoli
   or broccolini, ends trimmed and
   thicker stalks cut in half lengthways
200 g (7 oz) green beans,
   ends trimmed
200 g (7 oz) mange tout (snow peas)
1 small green courgette (zucchini),
   shaved into ribbons
1 small yellow courgette (zucchini),
   shaved into ribbons
5 large gherkins (pickles), thinly sliced
   lengthways
2 hass avocados, sliced

DRESSING

2 teaspoons dijon mustard
1 teaspoon caster (superfine) sugar
   or honey – optional
generous glug of white wine vinegar
juice of ½ lemon
generous glug of extra virgin olive oil

Preheat the oven to 180°C (350°F/gas mark 4). Place the whole spring onions in a roasting tin, drizzle with rapeseed oil and season with salt. Roast for 10–15 minutes or until golden.

Bring a large pan of salted water to the boil and add the broccoli and cauliflower. Cook for a minute or so, then add the purple sprouting broccoli or broccolini, green beans, mange tout and broccoli (you can do the vegetables in batches if your pan isn't large enough to hold them all at once). Cover and cook for 2–3 minutes or until the vegetables are crisp-tender. Drain the vegetables, then transfer to a large bowl or sink of iced water (or just really cold water, if adding ice seems a bit fussy). Blanching and refreshing vegetables in this way means they stay crisp and keep their vibrant colours – chill them in the fridge until you're ready to use them.

To make the dressing, combine all the ingredients in a jar, add salt and pepper to taste and shake well. Check the seasoning and adjust accordingly. This is a delicious, sharp but sweet dressing.

Place the blanched vegetables in a large serving bowl, along with the courgette ribbons, sliced gherkin and avocado. Pour over the dressing and toss until everything is generously coated. Finally, add the warm roasted spring onions and plenty of black pepper and serve straightaway.

TIP Use a vegetable peeler to shave the courgette into fine ribbons.

Preparation time: 5 minutes | **Cooking time:** 10 minutes | **Feeds:** 6

BASIL BUTTER CORN

Sometimes the simple dishes are the best dishes – and this is one of those dishes. Great as a snack or a side dish to a main meal.

6 corn cobs
handful of basil leaves
60 g (2¼ oz) soft butter
finely grated parmesan and lime
    wedges, to serve

Remove the papery husks and strands of silk from the corn cobs. Bring a large pan of salted water to the boil and cook for 5–8 minutes or until the corn kernels are just tender.

Meanwhile, use a pestle and mortar to pound the basil leaves to a paste with a pinch of salt. Add the butter and mix thoroughly.

Slather the cooked corn with the basil butter and sprinkle over a grinding of pepper, then serve with parmesan and lime wedges. Eat and enjoy every mouthful. Note that floss or toothpicks may be needed...

TIP To make this even better, barbecue the corn cobs in their husks. You'll need to soak them in water for 30 minutes beforehand, so they don't burn – this also helps keep the corn from drying out. Pull back the papery husks from the cobs and remove the silk, then brush the corn kernels with olive oil and season with salt. Re-cover the corn cobs with the husks and barbecue for 10–15 minutes, at a distance from the heat to avoid burning the husks.

Preparation time: 15 minutes | Cooking time: 3–4 hours | Feeds: 4–6

SWEET PORK & DATE RAGOUT

I've eaten this so many times in our favourite Argentinian restaurant in Paris, and I love it every time. Now I've mastered my own version with added toppings and crunch. Don't be put off by the long cooking time – no work is involved for most of it, as everything is thrown into a dish and slow-cooked. I cannot recommend this enough... just writing the recipe makes me hungry.

1 red onion, cut into quarters

1–2 ancho (dried poblano) chillies

4 cloves garlic, thinly sliced

2 bay leaves

1.75 litres (60 fl oz/7 cups) chicken stock

12 medjool dates, pitted

1 yellow courgette (zucchini), cut into 1 cm (½ in) rounds

3 teaspoons smoked paprika

1 x 400 g (14 oz) tin of tomatoes

1 kg (1 lb 2 oz) pork shoulder, trimmed of excess fat and cut into generous chunks (about 2.5 cm/1 in)

SALAD GARNISH

large handful of lamb's lettuce

5 medjool dates, pitted

1 red onion, thinly sliced

1 red chilli, thinly sliced

1 spring onion (scallion), thinly sliced

large handful of coriander (cilantro) leaves

glug of extra virgin olive oil

Preheat the oven to 170°C (325°F/gas mark 3).

In a large casserole or baking dish, combine the onion, dried chillies, garlic, bay leaves, stock, dates, courgette, paprika and tinned tomatoes. Add the pork, making sure the meat is well covered by the stock (add a splash of water if needed), then season with salt and pepper.

Cover and bake for 3–4 hours, giving everything a good stir after 2 hours. Keep an eye on the ragout during the last hour of cooking. You may need to add a splash of water if it seems dry, or take it out a little earlier if the meat is getting overcooked – you're aiming for fall-apart tender meat in a sweet, rich, dark sauce.

For your salad garnish, combine all the ingredients and season with salt and pepper, then pile on top of each generous serving of ragout.

TIP Be nice to your butcher, and they'll trim and cube the pork for you.

Preparation time: 10 minutes | **Cooking time:** 35 minutes | **Feeds:** 6–8

PEAR & STEM GINGER TARTE TATIN
WITH CARDAMOM CREAM

It wasn't until a little while back, at one of my pop-ups, that I started cooking with cardamom, and now I love its distinctive fragrance and warm nuttiness.

200 g (7 oz/1 cup) brown sugar

4 pears, peeled, cored and
    cut into 5 mm (¼ in) slices

2 balls of stem ginger (crystallised
    ginger in syrup), thinly sliced

1 vanilla pod (bean), cut in half
    and seeds scraped

1 roll (320 g/11¼ oz) ready-made
    puff pastry

1 tablespoon ground cardamom

300 ml (10½ fl oz) double (thick)
    cream or whipped cream

Preheat the oven to 180°C (350°F/gas mark 4).

Put the brown sugar in a baking dish or ovenproof frying pan and place over medium heat until the sugar has completely melted and caramelised. Do not move the pan or stir the sugar during this time – and don't be tempted to dip in a finger to try it, as the caramel gets seriously hot.

Arrange the pears neatly on top of the caramelised sugar, then sprinkle over the ginger slices and vanilla seeds and tuck in the vanilla pod. Cook for 5–6 minutes or until the pears start to soften.

Roll out the puff pastry so it's slightly bigger than your dish or pan, then place it on top of the pears, tucking in the sides. Transfer to the oven and bake or 15–20 minutes or until the pastry is golden and cooked through.

Meanwhile, fold the ground cardamom into the cream.

Remove the tarte tatin from the oven and let it stand for 30 seconds, then carefully turn out onto a plate. Serve in generous slices, with even more generous dollops of cardamom cream.

TIP If you can't find ground cardamom, pound cardamom pods to a powder using a pestle and mortar, then sieve to make sure you don't include any lumps; it's worth the effort, I promise.

Preparation time: 10 minutes | **Cooking time:** 20 minutes | **Feeds:** 4

STICKY PORK AND PINEAPPLE PAD THAI

This may seem like a long list of ingredients, but once you've built up your larder you'll more than likely have most of what you need, sauce and oil wise. For a vegetarian version, leave out the pork and the fish sauce.

350 g (12 oz) flat rice noodles
2 generous glugs of peanut or sesame oil
large handful of left-over cooked pork
1 teaspoon sugar
2 tablespoons pineapple juice
   (from the tinned pineapple)
generous pinch of chilli flakes
2 white onions, roughly chopped
3 cloves garlic, thinly sliced
2 red chillies, thinly sliced
7.5 cm (3 in) knob of ginger, peeled
   and finely shredded
1 carrot, peeled and cut into strips
   about 3 cm (1¼ in) long
1 x 225 g (8 oz) tin of bamboo shoots,
   drained
handful of pineapple chunks – tinned
   does the job
4 free-range eggs, lightly beaten
large glug of light soy sauce
large glug of fish sauce
juice of 2 limes

GARNISHES

4 spring onions (scallions), finely chopped
handful of roughly chopped coriander
   (cilantro)
1 red chilli, thinly sliced
chilli flakes
handful of coarsely ground peanuts

Place the noodles in a heatproof bowl and cover with boiling water from the kettle. Cover and leave for 15–20 minutes until the noodles are soft.

Pour a glug of oil into a large wok or frying pan. Place over high heat until the oil is almost smoking, then add the pork, sugar, pineapple juice and chilli flakes and fry for a few minutes until the meat is browned, then remove and set aside. Pour another glug of oil into the wok, then add the onions, garlic, chillies, ginger and carrot and stir-fry for 2–3 minutes – the vegetables should still have a bit of crunch. Stir in the bamboo shoots and pineapple, just to warm through, then remove the vegetable mixture from the wok and set aside.

Add the beaten egg to the wok, along with the soy sauce and fish sauce. Cook for a minute or so, using a spatula to break up the egg, then add the drained noodles, together with the fried pork and the vegetable mixture. Mix thoroughly – tongs are great for this. Squeeze over the lime juice and garnish with spring onions, coriander, chilli, chilli flakes and peanuts, then serve.

TIP Aside from the onion, garlic, ginger and chilli, the other veg are just suggestions, so feel free to use up any left-over courgettes (zucchini), peas, mange tout (snow peas), corn or spinach you have lying around, and to replace the pork with chicken or seafood if you like.

MAKE IT
FANCY
WEDNESDAYS

What a difference a day makes. By Wednesday, the weekend is in sight. Resist the urge to splash the cash on a dinner out and make your own fancy meals at home instead. Here there are tips on how to add a few restaurant-style touches to your home cooking. Plump for something Rustic or try your hand at something more Modern – whichever you choose, the aim here is to impress. Who you're impressing (and why) is up to you...

BREAKFAST
Pineapple & Gooey Coconut Macaroon Stack
with Honey & Greek Yogurt (v)
You're up early, early enough to treat yourself and go all out.

LUNCH
Nest of Radicchio with Tequila Scallop
& Coriander Ceviche
You've started as you mean to go on... keeping it fancy.

SNACK
Raw Corn Salsa with Parmesan Seeded
Blue Nachos (v)
Sticking with spice.

MODERN

DINNER
Crispy Buttermilk Chicken Tacos
with Onion & Radish Salsa
Wanting to impress and indulge at the same time.

DESSERT
Chocolate Orange Mousse with Pistachios (v)
Up for one last indulgence, why or how would you resist?!

LEFTOVERS
Buttermilk Chicken with Apricot Katsu Curry Sauce

(v) = vegetarian option

Preparation time: 10 minutes | **Cooking time:** 30 minutes | **Feeds:** 4–6 (makes 8–10 macaroons)

PINEAPPLE & GOOEY COCONUT MACAROON STACK WITH HONEY & GREEK YOGURT

This is a combination of all the things I love – the perfect start to any day in my book, and definitely one that's not to be missed. If you're going all out, some crumbled honeycomb makes a great addition.

4 egg whites
135 g (4¾ oz/1½ cups) desiccated coconut
145 g (5¼ oz/1½ cups) flaked almonds
165 g (5¾ oz/¾ cup) caster (superfine) sugar
2 tablespoons vanilla extract
½ pineapple, sliced
95 g (3¼ oz/⅓ cup) thick Greek-style yogurt
2 tablespoons runny honey
sprigs of mint, to serve

Preheat the oven to 180°C (350°F/gas mark 4) and line a baking sheet with baking paper.

In a heatproof bowl, combine the egg whites, coconut, almond flakes, sugar, vanilla extract and a teaspoon of salt. Set over a pan of simmering water – make sure the water isn't touching the base of the bowl – and cook for 7–8 minutes, stirring constantly, until the egg whites are opaque and the mixture is heated through.

Place generous tablespoons of the mixture onto the lined baking sheet, leaving plenty of space in between, as they'll flatten out when cooking. Bake for 5 minutes until they start to turn golden, then reduce the temperature to 170°C (325°F/gas mark 3) and cook for a further 10 minutes. Leave to cool before serving.

Stack the macaroons, layering them with pineapple and yogurt. Drizzle with honey and top with sprigs of mint, then serve immediately.

TIP If this requires a little too much effort in the morning, get the macaroons made the day before or at the weekend – they'll keep for 3–4 days in an airtight container.

Preparation time: 10 minutes | **Marinating time:** 30 minutes–1 hour | **Feeds:** 4–6

NEST OF RADICCHIO
WITH TEQUILA SCALLOP & CORIANDER CEVICHE

This tastes as good as it looks – fresh and zesty, with a chilli kick. When you buy the scallops, tell the fishmonger you're making ceviche, as they need to be really fresh.

500 g (1 lb 2 oz) super-fresh
   sustainable scallops
juice of 3 limes
dash of tequila
½ red onion, thinly sliced
½ red chilli, seeds removed, thinly sliced
1 grapefruit, cut into fine segments
small bunch of coriander (cilantro),
   roughly chopped
1 large radicchio, leaves separated
½ pomegranate, seeds only

Start by slicing the scallops into thin rounds (about three or four per scallop, depending on their thickness), then put them in a glass or ceramic bowl with the lime juice, tequila, onion and chilli. Add a sprinkle of salt and leave to marinate for between 30 minutes and 1 hour. During this time, the scallops will 'cook' in the lime juice and become opaque.

Taste for seasoning and adjust with extra lime juice or salt as needed. Add the grapefruit and half the coriander, then set aside for 5 minutes before serving.

Use a double layer of radicchio leaves to form 'nests' for the ceviche, then divide the scallops and grapefruit evenly between them, adding a dash of the marinating juices. Garnish with the remaining coriander and a sprinkling of the pomegranate seeds. Serve and eat immediately.

TIP To get the seeds out of a pomegranate, hold a pomegranate half cut-side down over a bowl, with your fingers spread out... Then use the back of a spoon to whack the back of the pomegranate and let the seeds fall through your fingers into the bowl.

Preparation time: 10 minutes | **Cooking time:** 5 minutes | **Feeds:** 6

RAW CORN SALSA WITH PARMESAN SEEDED BLUE NACHOS

For those days when you want a snack with some kick.

1 x 200 g (7 oz) bag of blue corn chips
50 g (1¾ oz) parmesan, finely grated
handful of mixed seeds, such as
    sesame, poppy and sunflower

RAW CORN SALSA
kernels from 3 corn cobs
1 red onion, finely diced
½–1 red chilli, seeds removed,
    finely diced
1 clove garlic, finely diced
handful of radishes, thinly sliced
generous glug of red wine vinegar
glug of extra virgin olive oil
handful of roughly chopped coriander
    (cilantro)
juice of 1 lime

Preheat the oven to 180°C (350°F/gas mark 4) and line a baking tray with baking paper.

Spread out the blue corn chips on the lined baking tray and scatter over the finely grated parmesan, followed by a light sprinkling of the mixed seeds. Bake for 3–5 minutes or until the parmesan starts to turn golden.

Place all the salsa ingredients in a serving bowl and mix thoroughly, seasoning to taste with salt and pepper.

Serve the nachos still warm from the oven, with the corn salsa for dipping.

Preparation time: 30 minutes | **Marinating time:** 1 hour – overnight |
Cooking time: 30 minutes | **Feeds:** 4 (or 2 with leftovers)

BUTTERMILK CHICKEN TACOS
WITH ONION & RADISH SALSA

Imagine moist, succulent chicken in a seriously crispy batter, and that's what you've got with this dish. Get involved.

450 g (1 lb) chicken thigh fillets,
    cut into bite-size chunks
300 g (10½ oz/2 cups) soy flour
    or plain (all-purpose) flour
1 teaspoon cayenne pepper
finely grated zest of ½ lemon
vegetable oil for deep-frying
4 soft flour tortillas
½ red cabbage, very finely shredded
½ bunch coriander (cilantro),
    finely chopped
1 red chill, thinly sliced

BUTTERMILK MARINADE
150 ml (5 fl oz) buttermilk
2 tablespoons smoked paprika
1 teaspoon cayenne pepper
2 tablespoons maple syrup

ONION & RADISH SALSA
1 large red onion, very thinly sliced
5 radishes, very thinly sliced
2.5 cm (1 in) knob of ginger, thinly sliced
¼ red chilli, thinly sliced
3 large glugs of red wine vinegar
1 tablespoon caster (superfine) sugar

PAPRIKA MAYO
4 tablespoons mayonnaise
1 tablespoon smoked paprika
glug of chilli sauce or Tabasco sauce
squeeze of lemon juice

Make the marinade by combining the buttermilk with the spices and maple syrup in a glass or ceramic bowl. Season with salt and pepper, then add the chicken and mix well. Cover and leave in the fridge to marinate for 1 hour or as long as your patience allows – overnight is best for flavour.

To make the onion and radish salsa, combine all the ingredients and set aside in the fridge for 15–20 minutes.

For the paprika mayo, combine all the ingredients in a bowl and season to taste.

When you're ready to cook the chicken, combine the flour with the cayenne and lemon zest in a shallow bowl, then season generously with salt and pepper.

Pour the vegetable oil into a deep-fryer or large heavy-based saucepan and heat to 190°C (375°F). If you don't have a thermometer, test the temperature by adding a cube of bread: it should sizzle and turn golden brown in 10 seconds.

Working in small batches, remove the chicken from the marinade, trying to keep as much marinade clinging to the meat as possible, then put it straight into the flour mixture, coating it well on all sides. Carefully add to the hot oil and deep-fry for 3–4 minutes until golden brown. Using a slotted spoon, remove the chicken from the oil and drain on paper towel.

To assemble the tacos, place a mound of shredded red cabbage in the middle of a tortilla, followed by a generous dollop of paprika mayo and a few pieces of the crispy fried buttermilk chicken. Top with the pickled onion and radish salsa, before garnishing with coriander and chilli.

TIP If you can't find buttermilk, substitute sour cream with a dash of milk.

CHOCOLATE ORANGE MOUSSE
WITH PISTACHIOS

If chocolate oranges are your chocolate treat of choice, this one's for you. If not, swap the oranges and Cointreau for honeycomb with Kahlua or Amaretto.

250 g (9 oz) dark chocolate

7 free-range eggs, separated

90 g (3¼ oz) caster (superfine) sugar

glug of Cointreau or other orange-flavoured liqueur

finely grated zest and juice of ½ orange

3 tablespoons cocoa powder

250 ml (9 fl oz/1 cup) double (thick) cream

200 g (7 oz) pistachios, roughly chopped

Break the chocolate into chunks and place in a heatproof bowl. Sit the bowl over a pan of simmering water, making sure the base of the bowl doesn't come into contact with the water, and stir until the chocolate has melted. Remove from the heat and leave to cool slightly.

Whisk the egg whites with a pinch of salt until they form stiff peaks. To test, try holding the bowl upside down if you're feeling brave – the whisked egg whites shouldn't budge.

In another bowl, combine the egg yolks with a pinch of salt, then add the sugar, Cointreau, orange zest and juice and 2 tablespoons of the cocoa powder. Whisk until the sugar dissolves completely, then pour in the cream and the melted chocolate and mix thoroughly. Finally, fold in the whisked egg whites – you want to keep as much air in the mousse as possible, so go gently! Keep folding until the mixture is a uniform colour and thoroughly combined.

Pour the mousse into one large serving bowl or individual dishes. Dust with the remaining cocoa powder, then sprinkle with pistachios. Chill for 1–2 hours to set before serving.

TIP Mix up the toppings for a change: try nut brittle, or fresh or dried fruit.

Preparation time: 10 minutes | **Cooking time:** 40 minutes | **Feeds:** 4

BUTTERMILK CHICKEN WITH APRICOT KATSU CURRY SAUCE

You'll be surprised how quickly you can get this dish together. I love a rich, full-flavoured homemade curry, and I'd choose this over a takeaway any day.

large handful of left-over buttermilk
   chicken (see page 79)
handful of roughly chopped coriander
   (cilantro)
1 spring onion (scallion), thinly sliced
   on the diagonal
steamed rice, to serve

CURRY SAUCE
glug of sesame oil or vegetable oil
1 white onion, roughly chopped
4 large cloves garlic, roughly chopped
5 cm (2 in) knob of ginger,
   finely chopped
1 carrot, peeled and roughly diced
1 tablespoon curry powder
1 teaspoon garam masala
2 heaped tablespoons plain
   (all-purpose) flour
500 ml (17 fl oz/2 cups) good-quality
   chicken stock
glug of dark soy sauce
1 tablespoon apricot jam

Preheat the oven to 190°C (375°F/gas mark 5).

Place the buttermilk chicken on a baking tray, cover with foil to prevent it drying out, then reheat it in the oven for 10–15 minutes or until warmed right through. Remove the foil and put the chicken under a hot grill (broiler) for 3–5 minutes to crisp it up.

For the curry sauce, pour a glug of oil into a saucepan over medium–low heat and add the onion, garlic, ginger and carrot. Cook for about 2–3 minutes until they start to soften, stirring every now and then – make sure the garlic doesn't burn. Sprinkle over the curry powder and garam masala and season with salt and pepper, then cook for a minute. Stir in the flour and cook for another minute.

Start to gradually add the chicken stock, stirring constantly. Once all the stock is in, you can increase the heat and boil the sauce for a few minutes to thicken, still stirring constantly. Add the soy sauce and apricot jam, then reduce the heat and simmer for 15 minutes to deepen the flavours. Taste for seasoning, adding pepper for extra heat or apricot jam for more sweetness. Either pass the sauce through a sieve or blitz in the pan with a stick blender until thick and smooth.

Pour the curry sauce over the chicken and garnish with coriander and spring onion. Serve with a big bowl of rice.

TIP If you're short on leftovers and time, just sprinkle breadcrumbs over slices of chicken breast fillet and bake them at 180°C (350°F/gas mark 4) for 10–12 minutes or until cooked through.

BREAKFAST
Harissa Fried Eggs (v)
You're pushed for time, but want something big on the flavour front.

LUNCH
Roasted Globe Artichokes with Baked Eggs & Parmesan (v)
You fancy something light but flavoursome for lunch.

SNACK
Garlic Fried Beef Tomatoes with Capers, Goat's Cheese & Grandad's Mint Sauce (v)
Ready for a treat?

RUSTIC

DINNER
On the BBQ Smoked Haddock Chowder
with Crispy Potatoes
The weather's held out...

DESSERT
Mum's Chocolate & Amaretti Brandy
Cream Crunch (v)
You've earned a serious mid-week treat.

LEFTOVERS
Smoked Haddock, Crispy Lardon & Corn Soup
in a Bread Bowl

(v) = vegetarian option

Preparation time: 5 minutes | **Cooking time:** 5 minutes | **Feeds:** 4

HARISSA FRIED EGGS

Most people seem to save eggs for a weekend brunch treat, choosing the easier option of cereal or toast before work. But this super-simple, delicious recipe is quick enough to whip up on any morning of the week.

glug of rapeseed oil

4 large free-range or organic eggs

100 g (3½ oz) pecorino or parmesan, roughly crumbled

3 tablespoons dried black olives, pitted

3 tomatoes (ideally green, yellow and orange varieties), cut into quarters

handful of roughly chopped flat-leaf parsley

handful of roughly chopped coriander (cilantro)

4 teaspoons harissa

crusty loaf of sourdough, to serve – optional

Start with a big glug of oil in a large non-stick frying pan and heat over medium–high heat for a minute or so. Crack in the eggs and sprinkle over the cheese and olives, then top with the tomatoes. Cook until the egg white has set and started to turn crispy at the edges, about 2–3 minutes. (To speed up the egg cooking process, cover the pan with a lid or foil.) Sprinkle over the parsley and coriander, dot with dollops of harissa and season generously with pepper.

Serve straight from the pan with big hunks of crusty sourdough, if you like, or just keep it carb-free.

Preparation time: 10 minutes | **Cooking time:** 1 hour | **Feeds:** 4

ROASTED GLOBE ARTICHOKES
WITH BAKED EGGS & PARMESAN

The distinct but delicate flavour of the globe artichoke is an unsung hero for me. Try this one and you'll feel like a pro, plus it looks like a real show-stopper.

4 globe artichokes
1 lemon
olive oil, for drizzling
smoked paprika, to garnish

GARLIC & TOMATO DRIZZLE
2 large cloves garlic, thinly sliced
1 red chilli, thinly sliced
sprinkle of chilli flakes
1 teaspoon smoked paprika
1 x 400 g (14 oz) tin of cherry tomatoes
handful of fresh cherry tomatoes
handful of finely chopped oregano

PARMESAN TOPPING
120 g (4¼ oz/2 cups) fresh
   breadcrumbs, ideally homemade
100 g (3½ oz) parmesan, finely grated
finely grated zest of 1 lemon
handful of chopped parsley

Preheat the oven to 190°C (375°F/gas mark 5) and bring a large saucepan of salted water to the boil.

To prepare your artichokes, cut off the stalks – make sure it's straight, so they'll stand up – then remove the tough outer leaves and trim 2–3 cm (¾–1¼ in) from the top, so there are no spiky bits left. Rinse, then put straight into a bowl of water with a squeeze of lemon juice added, to stop discolouration. When all the artichokes are done, put them in the pan of boiling water, adding another squeeze of lemon juice, and cook over medium–high heat for 15–20 minutes. When they're ready, they should be soft but not mushy. Transfer to a baking dish and drizzle generously with oil, then season with salt and pepper and roast for 30 minutes.

Meanwhile, in a pestle and mortar or a blender, combine the garlic with the fresh chilli, chilli flakes and paprika. Season with salt and pepper, then pound or blend to a rough paste. Pour a glug of oil into a pan over medium heat and cook the paste for a minute, stirring so it doesn't burn, then add the tinned and fresh cherry tomatoes and the oregano. Increase the heat to high and cook for 5–10 minutes until thick. Blitz with a stick blender, then taste and adjust the seasoning.

To make the parmesan topping, combine all the ingredients and season with pepper.

Once the artichokes have been in the oven for 30 minutes, drizzle over the sauce and sprinkle with the parmesan crust. Return the artichokes to the oven for 5 minutes until they just start to brown, then crack an egg into the centre of each one and bake for 3–4 minutes or until the egg is set and the breadcrumbs are golden. Garnish with an extra sprinkle of smoked paprika.

Preparation time: 10 minutes | **Cooking time:** 5 minutes | **Feeds:** 4

GARLIC FRIED BEEF TOMATOES
WITH CAPERS, GOAT'S CHEESE & GRANDAD'S MINT SAUCE

This dish couldn't be simpler. It's all about good produce: deep-red beef tomatoes, piquant capers and rich gooey goat's cheese, all pepped up with a dose of Grandad's famous mint sauce.

4 thick slices of sourdough

3 large beef (beefsteak) tomatoes, sliced

glug of olive oil

2 cloves garlic, thinly sliced

100 g (3½ oz) capers in vinegar, drained

small handful of finely shredded parsley

250 g (9 oz) goat's cheese, roughly crumbled

4 tablespoons white wine vinegar

glug of extra virgin olive oil

GRANDAD'S MINT SAUCE
bunch of fresh mint (ideally home-grown, as Grandad would use), leaves picked

1½ teaspoons granulated sugar

4 tablespoons malt vinegar

First make the mint sauce. Take a large knife and roughly chop the mint, then sprinkle over the sugar and chop the mint again. Add a dash of malt vinegar and chop again until the mint is finely chopped. Transfer to a bowl and gradually stir in the remaining vinegar, tasting as you go. Grandad says if it doesn't taste right, throw it away and start again. I say... adjust the vinegar and mint ratio, gradually add the vinegar and taste until you've got it just right – sharp, but sweet.

Lightly toast the sourdough. Season both sides of the tomato slices with salt and pepper. Heat a glug of olive oil in a frying pan over medium heat for a minute or so, then add the tomatoes and garlic and cook for 2–3 minutes, being careful not to let the garlic colour too much. Using a slotted spoon, remove the tomatoes and garlic from the pan, then dunk the toasted sourdough into the juices left in the pan, so it soaks them up. Top the sourdough with the fried tomatoes and garlic.

Combine the capers (add a glug of vinegar from the jar too, if you like), parsley, goat's cheese and white wine vinegar, then place on top of the tomatoes. Drizzle over the extra virgin olive oil and add a dollop of mint sauce.

TIP If you don't use all the mint sauce, store it in a jar in the fridge – it will keep for a day or two.

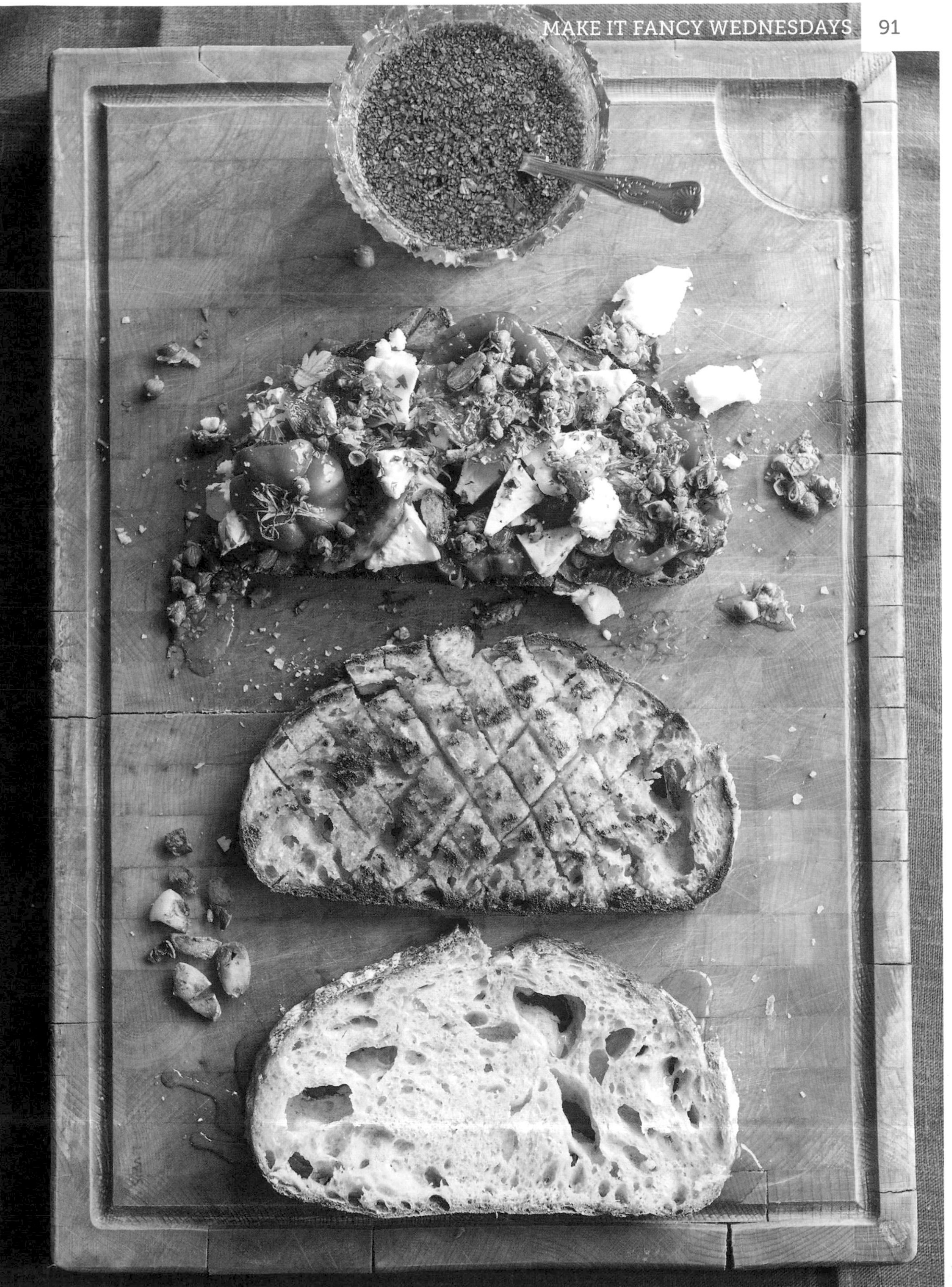

Preparation time: 10 minutes | **Cooking time:** 30 minutes | **Feeds:** 4 (or 2 with leftovers)

ON THE BBQ SMOKED HADDOCK CHOWDER WITH CRISPY POTATOES

Smoked haddock chowder has always been real comfort food for me, and a go-to dish when cooking for friends. It can be made just as easily on the hob, so don't let a rainy day put you off.

large knob of butter
1 white onion, diced
3 leeks, sliced
1 large carrot, grated
2 bay leaves
500 ml (17 fl oz/2 cups) fish stock
glug of white wine – optional
300 ml (10½ fl oz) crème fraîche
    (sour cream)
2 un-dyed smoked haddock fillets,
    pin-boned and cut into large chunks
1 lemon, cut into quarters
small handful of roughly chopped
    parsley

CRISPY POTATOES
glug of rapeseed oil
knob of butter
1 kg (2 lb 4 oz) new potatoes,
    cut into quarters
1 red onion, cut into wedges

If you're firing up the barbecue for this, get it up and running. You'll also need a large saucepan and a large frying pan or heavy-based skillet – make sure neither of them have any plastic parts, as they'll probably melt in the fierce heat of the barbecue. Cook the potatoes and chowder on the edge of the barbecue or on a higher shelf, then sear the fish and lemon on a grate closer to the coals.

For the potatoes, put the oil and butter into the frying pan or skillet over medium heat and add the potatoes and onion. Season with salt and cook for about 20–25 minutes until golden, turning occasionally.

Meanwhile, melt the butter in the saucepan over medium–low heat and add the onion, leeks, grated carrot and bay leaves. Season with salt and pepper, then cook until the onion and leeks have softened. Pour in the fish stock and white wine and let it boil for 6–8 minutes to deepen the flavours and cook off the alcohol. Add the crème fraîche and white pepper to taste, then simmer gently for about 5 minutes. Do not allow the chowder to boil or the crème fraîche may curdle – if this happens, remove from the heat and allow to cool slightly, then stir in a small knob of butter and you should be back on track.

Slide the fish chunks onto skewers, then lightly oil and season. Cook on the barbecue for 2–3 minutes or until the fish starts to turn opaque – be careful not to overcook. Quickly sear the lemon quarters until sweet and sticky.

If cooking on the hob, add the fish to the chowder and simmer for 2–3 minutes. Remove from the heat and let the fish poach in the hot chowder for a further 1–2 minutes.

Ladle the chowder into bowls, then sprinkle with parsley and serve with the barbecued fish and crispy potatoes.

Preparation time: 30 minutes | **Cooking time:** 10 minutes | **Chilling time:** 2 hours | **Feeds:** 6–8

MUM'S CHOCOLATE & AMARETTI BRANDY CREAM CRUNCH

Like a few of the other desserts I've included in the book, this takes me right back to my greedy childhood. Mum would cook this the day before she was having a dinner party, and it would sit there in its fancy crystal glass bowl in the fridge, tempting us.

500 ml (17 fl oz/2 cups) double (thick) cream
1 tablespoon icing (confectioners') sugar
350 g (12 oz) amaretti biscuits
90 ml (3 fl oz) brandy

CHOCOLATE SAUCE
300 g (10½ oz) good-quality dark chocolate
455 ml (16 fl oz) double (thick) cream
1 tablespoon cocoa powder

For the chocolate sauce, break the dark chocolate into chunks, then melt in a heatproof bowl set over a pan of simmering water (make sure the base of the bowl isn't touching the water).

In a separate pan, heat the cream until it is warm to the touch (don't let it boil). Pour the cream into the bowl of melted chocolate, then add the cocoa powder and a sprinkle of salt and whisk until it all comes together to make a thick, rich sauce. Set aside to cool for 10–20 minutes.

Meanwhile, whisk the cream with the icing sugar until it forms soft peaks.

To assemble the dessert, take a large serving bowl or cake tin and place a layer of amaretti biscuits in the base, leaving no gaps. Drizzle over about 1½ tablespoons of the brandy – this will make the biscuits gooey and delicious. Next spoon over the cooled chocolate sauce, followed by a layer of the whipped cream. Repeat these layers until all the ingredients have been used up. Refrigerate for a couple of hours, so it's thoroughly chilled and set.

Be generous when serving – although this is super-rich, I'd be devastated if I got a mean portion!

TIP Make sure the chocolate sauce has completely cooled before layering it with the cream.

Preparation time: 10 minutes | **Cooking time:** 20 minutes | **Feeds:** 4

SMOKED HADDOCK, CRISPY LARDON & CORN SOUP IN A BREAD BOWL

Just when you're wondering what you should do with the left-over chowder... This is so good, and there's a childish part of me that loves it all the more because it's served in a bread bowl. Not into carbs? Look away now! Or serve in a regular bowl, but you'll be missing out.

4 small round crusty bread rolls
glug of olive oil
180 g (6¼ oz) smoked lardons
2 corn cobs
knob of butter
2 tablespoons plain (all-purpose) flour
500 ml (17 fl oz/2 cups) milk
500 ml (17 fl oz/2 cups) fish stock
about 250 ml (1 cup) left-over smoked
   haddock chowder (see page 93) or
   1 un-dyed smoked haddock fillet,
   pin-boned and skin removed,
   chopped into chunks
small handful of roughly chopped
   parsley

Preheat the oven to 180°C (350°F/gas mark 4).

Slice off the tops of your bread rolls, so you have lids for your soup bowls. Hollow out the insides (you can add the bread to the soup if you like, or roast chunks of it to make croutons), then drizzle olive oil into the hollowed-out rolls and roast in the oven for 6–8 minutes – this will stop your bread bowl from leaking.

Fry the smoked lardons over high heat until golden and crisp. Using a sharp knife, carefully slice the corn kernels from the cobs and add to the pan with the lardons. Cook for a minute, then remove the lardons and corn from the pan and set aside. Reduce the heat to medium–low and add a knob of butter to the pan. When the butter has melted, add the flour and a sprinkle of pepper and stir until it forms a paste. Gradually add the milk and fish stock, stirring constantly, until the soup is thick and smooth.

Return the lardons and corn to the pan and simmer for a few minutes to re-heat, then add the left-over chowder and warm through. If you're using smoked haddock rather than left-over chowder, add it the soup and simmer for 2–3 minutes, then remove from the heat and let the fish poach in the hot soup for a further 2–3 minutes.

Taste for seasoning and adjust accordingly. Sprinkle with parsley and pour into the bread bowls.

COOKING FOR COMPANY THURSDAYS

Thursdays should be sociable. You're close enough to the weekend to handle a hangover or a late night, so why not start the weekend early? Cook for your housemates, your family, your friends, or even the dog. The fact is, most of us will be cooking after work, and these recipes will help you to do just that. Choose between Homely & Hearty and Faraway Flavours, then cheat your way around cooking for larger groups – no special skills needed! Robust and delicious, these meals are perfect for sharing, and if you're short on time you can rope people in to help.

BREAKFAST
Breakfast Porridge Crème Brûlée (v)
You're in a caring, sharing mood.

LUNCH
Sticky & Sweet Bruschetta (v)
Fancy something sweet, fresh and easily shareable?

SNACK
Whole Roast Cauliflower with Gorgonzola Sauce & Garlic Dippers (v)
After something hot with bold, rich flavours? This is the dish for you...

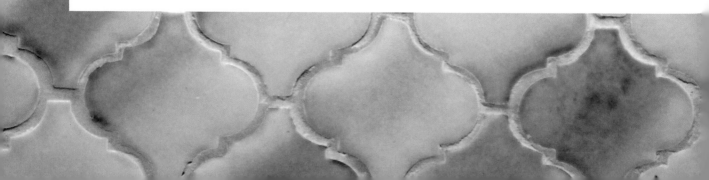

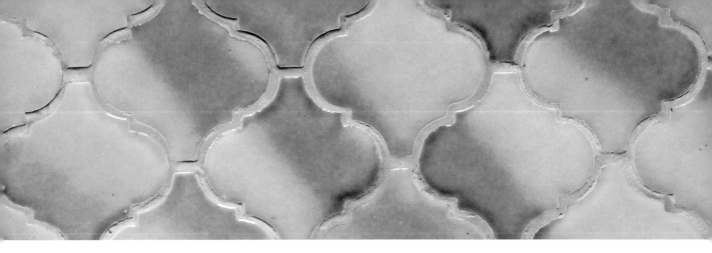

HOMELY&HEARTY

DINNER
Cheat's Chicken Kiev Cordon Bleu Style
with Caperberry Slaw
Keen to make sure everyone's full?

DESSERT
Chocolate & Guinness Date Cake with White Chocolate
& Lemon Topping (v)
Up for one last indulgence, why or how would you resist!

LEFTOVERS
The Pimped Up KO Sarnie

(v) = vegetarian option

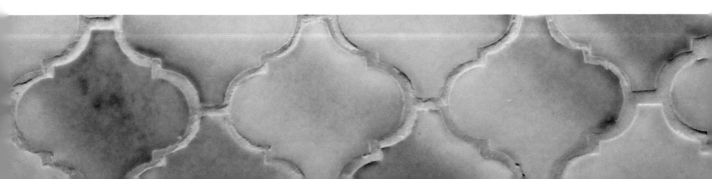

Preparation time: 2 minutes | **Cooking time:** 10 minutes | **Feeds:** 1

BREAKFAST PORRIDGE
CRÈME BRÛLÉE

Sometimes it's the simple things that are the most comforting. This half-breakfast, half-dessert combo makes the perfect morning treat.

50 g (1¾ oz/½ cup) rolled
    (porridge) oats
350 ml (12 fl oz) whole milk
dollop of thick coconut yogurt
    or regular yogurt
drizzle of honey
sprinkle of caster (superfine) sugar

Put the oats and milk into a pan, along with a pinch of salt. Bring to the boil, then turn the heat down to low and cook for 4–5 minutes, stirring every now and then to make sure the porridge doesn't stick to the bottom of the pan.

Once the porridge is cooked and creamy, transfer to a heatproof bowl. Add a dollop of yogurt and a drizzle of honey, then sprinkle over a thin layer of sugar. Use a kitchen blow-torch or place under a very hot grill (broiler) to melt the sugar until it caramelises and becomes brittle.

TIP For a leaner option, use a mixture of water and semi-skimmed milk or almond milk – and perhaps leave out the sugar topping!

Preparation time: 15 minutes | **Cooking time:** 5–10 minutes| **Feeds:** 6–8

STICKY & SWEET BRUSCHETTA

This is bruschetta with a little twist. Who doesn't like bruschetta?

1 loaf of Turkish bread, cut in half
   lengthways
2 big glugs of extra virgin olive oil,
   plus extra for drizzling
5 large cloves garlic, 3 thinly sliced,
   2 cut in half lengthways
1 red onion, thinly sliced
350 g (12 oz) cherry tomatoes,
   cut into quarters
2 large handfuls of basil leaves,
   roughly torn, plus extra to garnish
100 ml (3½ fl oz) red wine vinegar
200 g (7 oz) physalis
   (cape gooseberries)

Preheat the oven to 180°C (350°F/gas mark 4).

Drizzle the bread with olive oil, then place on a baking tray and toast in the oven for 5–10 minutes until golden.

Meanwhile, for the topping, combine the finely sliced garlic, onion, tomatoes, basil, vinegar and olive oil in a bowl. Season generously with salt and pepper to taste.

Rub the cut side of the halved garlic cloves over the toasted bread, then pile on the topping, covering all corners so no one gets short-changed.

Garnish with the physalis, an extra sprinkle of basil and a generous drizzle of olive oil, plus any tomato juices from the bowl. Cut into slices to serve or leave as one giant bruschetta to be torn and shared.

TIP Add prosciutto for the meat-lovers.

Preparation time: 10 minutes | **Cooking time:** 30 minutes | **Feeds:** 4–6

WHOLE ROAST CAULIFLOWER
WITH GORGONZOLA SAUCE & GARLIC DIPPERS

Flavour-wise, this is a match made in heaven. Even committed carnivores won't notice the lack of meat here.

1 whole cauliflower, leaves left on
glug of olive oil

GORGONZOLA SAUCE
20 g (¾ oz) butter
½ teaspoon English mustard
2 tablespoons plain (all-purpose) flour
250 ml (9 fl oz/1 cup) semi-
　skimmed milk
125 g (4½ oz) gorgonzola, crumbled
handful of cashews, half ground,
　half coarsely crushed

GARLIC DIPPERS
1–2 large cloves garlic, cut in half
　lengthways
3 slices of wholegrain seeded bread
big glug of olive oil

Preheat the oven to 190°C (375°F/gas mark 5).

Place the whole cauliflower in a baking dish or roasting tin. Drizzle with olive oil and season well with salt and pepper, then roast for 15–20 minutes or until golden and tender.

Meanwhile, to make the garlic dippers, rub the cut side of a garlic clove over both sides of the bread, then cut the bread into fingers about 1.5 cm (⅝ in) wide. Heat the oil in a frying pan over medium heat and cook the bread fingers until golden, turning them once. For extra garlic flavour, finely chop another garlic clove and add it to the frying pan 30 seconds prior to serving.

For the sauce, melt the butter in a saucepan over medium–low heat then whisk in the mustard and flour. Season with salt and pepper, then gradually add the milk, whisking all the time, until you have a smooth, thick sauce. Add three-quarters of the gorgonzola and whisk until it melts into the sauce, then taste and adjust the seasoning as needed.

Pour the sauce over the roasted cauliflower, then scatter over the remaining gorgonzola and the cashews. Return to the oven for 5–7 minutes or until the cheese and cashews have browned. Serve straightaway, with garlic dippers on hand to mop up all the sauce.

Preparation time: 20 minutes | **Cooking time:** 35 minutes | **Feeds:** 6 (or 2–4 with leftovers)

CHEAT'S CHICKEN KIEV CORDON BLEU STYLE WITH CAPERBERRY SLAW

I love homemade chicken kiev, especially with this piquant caperberry slaw. It's my guilty pleasure. Just buy good meat and don't scrimp on the garlic.

125 g (4½ oz) mozzarella,
   cut into six slices
3 large chicken breasts on the bone,
   cut in half, skin removed
6 slices of prosciutto
whole bulb of garlic, cloves separated
glug of rapeseed oil

BREADCRUMB TOPPING
3 slices of brown or white bread
60 g (2¼ oz) parmesan, finely grated
4 tablespoons crispy shallots
finely grated zest of 1 lemon
handful of finely chopped parsley

CAPERBERRY SLAW
1 small red cabbage, finely shredded
1 small white cabbage, finely shredded
1 x 250 g (9 oz) jar of caperberries
   in vinegar
3 tablespoons salad cream or
   mayonnaise – optional

Preheat the oven to 190°C (375°F/gas mark 5).

Place a slice of mozzarella on top of each piece of chicken, then wrap the chicken in a slice of prosciutto. Place all the wrapped chicken in a baking dish, with the mozzarella side facing upwards. Add the garlic cloves, tucking them in between the chicken pieces, before adding a generous drizzle of oil and a decent pinch of salt and pepper. Cook in the oven for 12–15 minutes or until the prosciutto starts to go crispy.

Blitz the bread in a food processor or chop it with a knife to make coarse breadcrumbs. Transfer to a bowl and combine with the parmesan, crispy shallots, lemon zest and parsley, then season to taste with salt and pepper.

Cover the chicken pieces with the breadcrumbs and return to the oven for a further 12–20 minutes until the breadcrumbs are golden and crispy.

Meanwhile, for the caperberry slaw, combine the red and white cabbage with the drained caperberries, then add a glug of vinegar from the jar and season generously with salt and pepper. For a slightly more indulgent version, stir through the salad cream or mayonnaise (I'm a salad cream girl).

Serve the chicken with the caperberry slaw on the side.

TIP Look for ready-made crispy shallots at Asian supermarkets, or make your own by frying up thinly sliced shallots until crisp and golden.

Preparation time: 10 minutes | Cooking time: 1 hour | Feeds: 8–10

CHOCOLATE & GUINNESS DATE CAKE WITH WHITE CHOCOLATE & LEMON TOPPING

This is one cake you can't go wrong with – plus it can last all week, so no need to scoff it all at once...

250 ml (9 fl oz/1 cup) Guinness

300 g (10½ oz) unsalted butter

330 g (11¾ oz/1½ cups) caster (superfine) sugar

80 g (2¾ oz/¾ cup) cocoa powder

2 free-range eggs

150 ml (5 fl oz) sour cream

1 tablespoon vanilla extract

2 teaspoons baking powder

300 g (10½ oz/2 cups) plain (all-purpose) flour

250 g (9 oz) pitted dates, roughly chopped

WHITE CHOCOLATE TOPPING

300 g (10½ oz) good-quality white chocolate

finely grated zest of 1 lemon

1 tablespoon poppy seeds

Preheat the oven to 190°C (375°F/gas mark 5). Lightly butter a 23–25 cm (9–10 in) cake tin and line with baking paper.

Put the Guinness and butter in a large saucepan over medium–low heat. When the butter has melted and the Guinness has warmed through, take off the heat and whisk in the sugar and cocoa.

In a bowl, whisk the eggs with the sour cream and vanilla extract, then add to the pan, along with the baking powder, flour and salt. Whisk thoroughly until all the lumps are gone, then stir in the dates. Transfer to the prepared cake tin and bake for 45–55 minutes or until the cake has risen and is no longer wobbly in the centre. Leave to cool in the tin.

For the white chocolate topping, break up the chocolate and place in a heatproof bowl. Melt over a pan of simmering water – ensure that the bowl isn't touching the water – then stir in the lemon zest.

Carefully remove the cooled cake from the tin and place on a wire rack with a tray or plate underneath (to catch any drips). Pour the white chocolate topping over the cake, then sprinkle with the poppy seeds and leave to set.

Stored in an airtight container, this cake will last up to a week... in theory, at least.

TIP For an extra zesty finish, garnish the cake with freshly grated lemon zest.

Preparation time: 10 minutes | **Feeds:** 1

THE PIMPED UP KO SARNIE

This recipe comes from a time when I worked for Kelly Osbourne, and used to make a simpler version of this chicken sandwich for her lunch everyday. Here's how to really go all out with a chicken sarnie...

½–1 left-over chicken kiev (see page 109), cut into bite-size pieces
2 slices of good-quality seeded bread

DRESSING
25 g (1 oz/¼ cup) finely grated parmesan
generous dollop of mayonnaise
½ teaspoon finely grated lemon zest
½ teaspoon dijon mustard
small dash of red wine vinegar
2 teaspoons capers, roughly chopped
handful of finely chopped parsley
1 baby gem (cos) lettuce, leaves separated

Preheat the oven to 180°C (350°F/gas mark 4).

Wrap the left-over chicken kiev in foil and warm in the oven until heated through – this should take about 5–7 minutes.

Meanwhile, in a large bowl, combine the parmesan, mayonnaise, lemon zest, mustard, vinegar, capers and parsley, then season with salt and pepper. Add the lettuce leaves and toss to coat.

Stack the chicken and the dressed lettuce leaves on one slice of bread, drizzling over any extra dressing left in the bowl. Place the other slice of bread on top, then get your chops around it and enjoy.

TIP Add an anchovy or two to take this sarnie to the next level.

BREAKFAST
Muffin Tinned Huevos Rancheros (v)
Feeling adventurous?

LUNCH
Tuna Ceviche in Fried Tacos with Avocado & Pickled Ginger
Going light(ish) with lunch after a filling breakfast.

SNACK
Tempura Chilli Squid
Got a bit of time to get your cook on?

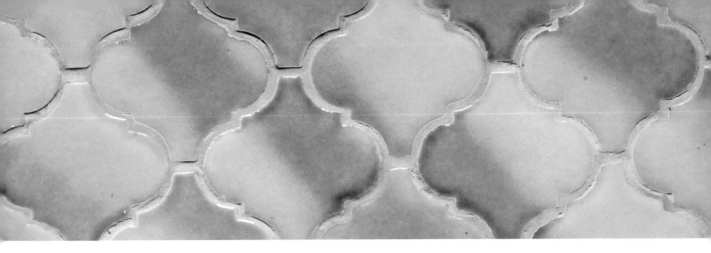

FARAWAYFLAVOURS

DINNER

South of the Border Spread:
Steak with South American Style Salsa Verde
Sour Cream, Coriander & Paprika Tats (v)
Roasted Spring Onions (v)
Gruyère Corn Gratin with Broccoli Dippers (v)

Feeling the pressure to please everyone? Bring it out buffet-style.

DESSERT

Rosemary & Almond Alfajores (v)

Sticking with the theme.

LEFTOVERS

Shredded Spring Onion, Corn Gratin, Salsa Verde
& Smoked Cheese Toastie (v)

(v) = vegetarian option

Preparation time: 10 minutes | **Cooking time:** 15 minutes | **Feeds:** 6

MUFFIN TINNED HUEVOS RANCHEROS

I served this up as a vegetarian starter at one of my pop-ups and the meat-eaters were jealous. This never fails to impress. Even better, you can get prepped in advance if you want some time to enjoy breakfast yourself.

3 soft flour tortillas, cut in half
6 free-range eggs
150 g (5½ oz) lamb's lettuce
80 g (2¾ oz) feta, crumbled
150 ml (5 fl oz) sour cream
sprinkle of smoked paprika
1–2 jalapeños, sliced

SMOKY TOMATOES
1 large clove garlic, thinly sliced
1 x 400 g (14 oz) tin of tomatoes
½ teaspoon smoked paprika
sprinkle of finely chopped oregano

GRUYÈRE SAUCE
50 g (1¾ oz) salted butter
½ teaspoon English mustard
2 tablespoons plain (all-purpose) flour
350 ml (12 fl oz) semi-skimmed milk
70 g (2½ oz) gruyère, grated

Preheat the oven to 180°C (350°F/gas mark 4).

For the smoky tomatoes, place all the ingredients in a pan and season with salt and pepper. Leave to cook over medium heat while you make the gruyère sauce.

To make the gruyère sauce, melt the butter in a small saucepan over medium–low heat, then whisk in the mustard and flour and keep stirring until it forms a paste. Gradually add the milk, stirring constantly, until you have a thick sauce. Add the cheese, season with salt and pepper and keep stirring until the cheese melts to make a smooth, lump-free sauce.

Take a six-hole 250 ml (1 cup) non-stick muffin tin and press half a tortilla into each hole. Bake in the oven for about 3 minutes, then add a spoonful of the smoky tomatoes, followed by a dollop of cheesy sauce and an egg yolk, plus a little of the egg white, being careful that it doesn't spill over the sides. Bake for 5–10 minutes until the tortillas start to crisp but the egg yolks are still runny.

Garnish with lamb's lettuce, a few dots of feta and sour cream, a sprinkling of paprika and some slices of jalapeño. Season with salt and pepper, then serve immediately.

TIP Add the egg yolk first, then just a little of the white, so it won't spill over the sides in the oven. You can use any left-over egg white to make macaroons (see page 72).

Preparation time: 15 minutes | **Cooking time:** 10 minutes | **Feeds:** 6

TUNA CEVICHE IN FRIED TACOS WITH AVOCADO & PICKLED GINGER

This makes a perfect light lunch: super-fresh, with interesting textures and delicate flavours.

30 wonton wrappers

vegetable oil for deep-frying

2 hass avocados

1 tablespoon crème fraîche
    (sour cream)

small glug of sesame oil

3 limes, 2 cut into quarters, 1 juiced

1 large spring onion (scallion),
    thinly sliced on the diagonal

1 x 190 g (6¾ oz) jar of pickled ginger,
    drained

1 green chilli, finely diced

350 g (12 oz) sashimi-grade sustainable
    tuna, cut into fine strips

Start by deep-frying the wonton wrappers. Pour a 2 cm (1 in) depth of oil into a large wok or frying pan and heat to 180°C (350°F). If you don't have a thermometer, check the oil is hot enough by adding a test wrapper – it should sizzle and float to the top. Working in batches, deep-fry the wonton wrappers for about a minute until crisp and golden, then carefully remove from the oil and drain on paper towel. Pile onto a plate or tray to serve.

In a bowl, combine the avocado, crème fraîche, sesame oil and lime juice. Season with white pepper, then mash to a smooth-ish consistency. Transfer to a serving bowl. Place the prepared spring onion, ginger and chilli in separate small serving bowls.

Arrange the tuna strips on a plate or platter, then set everything out and let people help themselves. The idea is to place a little bit of everything between two wonton wrappers, then squeeze a lime quarter over the tuna and get it in your gob...

Preparation time: 10 minutes | Cooking time: 15 minutes | Feeds: 4

TEMPURA CHILLI SQUID

I don't think I know anyone who doesn't cave at tempura squid, and this punchy dipping sauce is the perfect accompaniment. I could eat endless amounts of it. If you find you feel the same way, I'd double my already generous recipe, just to make sure you're not left short.

sunflower oil for deep-frying
600 g (1 lb 5 oz) squid, scored and cut
    into 5–6 strips, including tentacles
lemon wedges, to serve

BATTER
120 g (4¼ oz) plain (all-purpose) flour
120 g (4¼ oz) cornflour (cornstarch)
5 egg whites
300 ml (10½ fl oz) cold sparkling water
small sprinkle of finely chopped
    coriander (cilantro)

DIPPING SAUCE
generous glug of sesame oil
3 tablespoons rice wine vinegar
3 tablespoons light soy sauce
1 red chilli, thinly sliced
small pinch of finely chopped
    coriander (cilantro)
2 teaspoons finely chopped
    pickled ginger
1 teaspoon palm sugar or
    caster (superfine) sugar
½ spring onion (scallion),
    finely chopped

In a large bowl, whisk together all the batter ingredients until smooth, seasoning with salt and pepper.

Make the dipping sauce by combining all the ingredients in a small serving bowl. Taste it to make sure the sugar is fully dissolved and that you've got the sweet versus tangy balance just right.

Pour the sunflower oil into a deep-fryer or large heavy-based saucepan and heat to 190°C (375°F) or until a drop of the batter added to the oil sizzles and floats to the top straightaway.

Working in small batches, dip the squid strips into the batter and deep-fry for 1–2 minutes or until golden and cooked through. Drain on paper towel, then serve with lemon wedges and the dipping sauce.

Preparation time: 20 minutes | **Cooking time:** 5 minutes | **Resting time:** 5 minutes | **Feeds:** 6

STEAK WITH SOUTH AMERICAN STYLE SALSA VERDE

It's hard to beat a buffet-style spread for effortless entertaining: pick and mix from the sides over the page, put it all on the table and relax. This steak is always a winning dish – just be careful not to overcook the meat, then let it rest, and you'll love every mouthful.

6 x 280 g (10 oz) best-quality fillet
   or sirloin steaks
olive oil for frying

SALSA VERDE
2 cloves garlic, crushed
handful of capers
handful of cornichons
large handful of parsley leaves
large handful of coriander
   (cilantro) leaves
large handful of mint leaves
1 rounded tablespoon dijon mustard
generous glug of red wine vinegar
even more generous glug of
   extra virgin olive oil

Take the steaks out of the fridge about an hour beforehand, so they're at room temperature.

Meanwhile, for the salsa verde, finely chop all the ingredients and mix thoroughly. Season to taste with salt and black and white pepper.

When you're ready to cook the steaks, season them on both sides with salt and pepper. Heat a glug of olive oil in a frying pan or skillet over high heat. Add the steaks and cook for around 35–45 seconds, then flip them over. Continue to flip the steaks every 35–45 seconds until they've been cooking for around 3 minutes in total, depending on their thickness; if your steaks are thicker than 5 cm (2 in), add a bit of extra time. This will give you rare steak. If you want medium-rare, cook for another 30 seconds on each side.

Leave the steaks to rest for at least 5 minutes, then serve with large dollops of salsa verde.

TIP You can also slice up the steaks and share them, halving the amount of meat you need to buy... it's just as nice this way.

Preparation time: 10 minutes | **Cooking time:** 45 minutes | **Feeds:** 6

SOUR CREAM, CORIANDER & PAPRIKA TATS

Just so you've got all bases covered. No one can resist a roast potato...
Add spice, sour cream and coriander and there's no chance.

1 kg (2 lb 4 oz) new potatoes or
   desiree potatoes, roughly cut
   into 1.5 cm (⅝ in) cubes
generous glug of olive oil
1 heaped tablespoon smoked paprika
bunch of coriander (cilantro),
   roughly chopped
200 g (7 oz) sour cream

Preheat the oven to 200°C (400°F/gas mark 6).
    Bring a pan of salted water to the boil, then add the potatoes and cook for 8–10 minutes until they soften slightly – they should easily slip off a knife if prodded.
    Drain, then tip into an oiled roasting tin and sprinkle with salt and smoked paprika. Roast for 25 minutes, then check to see if they're golden and crispy. If not, shake the tin and roast them for another 5–10 minutes.
    Transfer to a serving bowl, stir in the coriander and top with dollops of sour cream.

Preparation time: 2 minutes | **Cooking time:** 15 minutes | **Feeds:** 6

ROASTED SPRING ONIONS

A side dish that should not be left out, take my word for it.

12–15 spring onions (scallions), ends
   trimmed – but leave the darker
   green outer layers intact
glug of rapeseed oil

Preheat the oven to 200°C (400°F/gas mark 6).
    Put the spring onions in a roasting tin and drizzle with rapeseed oil. Season with salt and pepper, then roast for 10–15 minutes or until soft and starting to turn golden.

Preparation time: 15 minutes | **Cooking time:** 40 minutes | **Feeds:** 6

GRUYÈRE CORN GRATIN WITH BROCCOLI DIPPERS

This has been tried and tested many a time – it's a genuine crowd-pleaser. Once you've tasted it, there will be no turning back.

3 corn cobs
60 g (2¼ oz) butter
1 teaspoon English mustard
50 g (1¾ oz/⅓ cup) plain (all-purpose) flour
500 ml (17 fl oz/2 cups) semi-skimmed milk
½ white onion, diced
2 cloves garlic, finely chopped
100 g (3½ oz/1 cup) grated gruyère
handful of finely chopped coriander (cilantro)
handful of rustic breadcrumbs, ideally from a baguette

BROCCOLI DIPPERS

350 g (12 oz) purple sprouting broccoli or broccolini, trimmed and stalks cut in half lengthways if thick
glug of extra virgin olive oil
finely grated zest and juice of ½ lemon

Preheat the oven to 180°C (350°F/gas mark 4).

Use a sharp knife to slice the corn kernels from the cobs – careful of your fingers – then set aside.

Melt the butter in a saucepan over medium heat and whisk in the mustard and flour until a thick paste starts to form. Season with salt, then gradually add the milk, stirring constantly. Keep stirring and cooking until you have a thick, rich sauce.

Add the corn kernels, onion, garlic and most of the gruyère, saving a small handful to sprinkle over the top. Stir until the cheese has melted, then add the coriander and transfer to a large baking dish (or a couple of smaller dishes, depending what you have in your kitchen). Top with the breadcrumbs and the remaining cheese, then bake for 20–25 minutes or until golden brown and bubbling.

Meanwhile, make the broccoli dippers. Pour a splash of water into a frying pan, just enough to cover the base, then add the broccoli and cover with a lid or foil, so the broccoli steams. Cook for around 3–4 minutes, adding a little more water if it evaporates too soon – the broccoli should remain crisp and firm and be a vibrant green colour. Drain off any water that's left in the pan, then add the olive oil, lemon juice and zest, and salt and pepper to taste. Toss the broccoli to coat.

Serve the gratin straight from the oven, with the broccoli dippers on the side.

Preparation time: 30 minutes | Chilling time: 1 hour | Cooking time: 30 minutes | Feeds: 10

ROSEMARY & ALMOND ALFAJORES

With subtle and delicious flavours, these are an extravagant accompaniment to an after-dinner or mid-morning coffee – to be enjoyed when you fancy indulging. To go all out, roll the alfajores in grated chocolate and/or chopped mixed nuts (pistachios add a burst of colour) instead of ground almonds.

110 g (3¾ oz/¾ cup) plain
   (all-purpose) flour
125 g (4½ oz/1 cup) cornflour
   (cornstarch)
½ teaspoon baking powder
4 large sprigs of rosemary
75 g (2½ oz/⅓ cup) granulated sugar
250 g (9 oz) unsalted butter
2 large egg yolks
small glug of pisco or brandy
2 teaspoons vanilla extract
150 g (5½ oz/1½ cups) ground almonds
   (almond meal)
310 g (11 oz/1 cup) dulce de leche

Combine the flour, cornflour, baking powder and a pinch of salt in a bowl.

Strip the leaves from the rosemary stalks into a mortar, then add the sugar and grind with the pestle. Transfer to a food processor or the bowl of an electric mixer, then add the butter and beat until it's light and fluffy. Add the egg yolks, pisco or brandy and vanilla extract and beat until thoroughly mixed.

Now you're ready to start adding the flour mixture. Do this gradually (on a low speed if using a mixer) until a dough forms. Wrap the dough in plastic wrap and chill in the fridge for about an hour.

Preheat the oven to 180°C (350°F/gas mark 4) and line two baking trays with baking paper. Lightly flour your work surface and roll out the dough to a thickness of about 1.5 cm (⅝ in). Using a 5 cm (2 in) round pastry cutter or the rim of a small glass, cut out 20 discs. Place on the prepared baking trays, spacing them out well, then bake for 12–15 minutes or until pale and firm. Transfer to a wire rack to cool.

Scatter the ground almonds over a plate or tray. Spread a generous teaspoon of dulce de leche on the underside of half of the discs, then place the other discs on top to make alfajores. Coat the sides with more dulce de leche, then roll in the ground almonds to coat. Eat straightaway or store in an airtight container somewhere cool (but not the fridge), so the dulce de leche doesn't melt and ooze out – they should last a good few days.

Preparation time: 5 minutes | **Cooking time:** 5 minutes | **Feeds:** 1

SHREDDED SPRING ONION, CORN GRATIN, SALSA VERDE & SMOKED CHEESE TOASTIE

If, like me, you hate throwing food away, then this is the perfect way to use up all those left-over bits and create a great new combination of flavours at the same time.

1 tablespoon left-over gruyère corn gratin (see page 125)

2 slices of sourdough bread

1 generous teaspoon left-over salsa verde (see page 123)

½ roasted spring onion (see page 124), shredded

70 g (2½ oz/⅔ cup) scamorza or other smoked cheese, grated

butter – optional

Spread the corn gratin over one slice of bread, then add the salsa verde, followed by the shredded spring onion. Heap the grated cheese in the middle, then press the other slice of bread on top. If you're not watching your waistline, lightly butter the outside of your toastie.

Add the toastie to a hot frying pan and cook over medium–low heat until golden on one side, then flip over and cook the other side until golden. Check the cheese has properly melted before removing the toastie from the pan; if not, turn down the heat and cook for a moment longer.

Wait a minute before stuffing it straight in... hot cheese can be seriously hot.

BARELY IN THE KITCHEN FRIDAYS

Fridays are usually hectic, so these are quick dishes that can be thrown together without too much effort or time in the kitchen. Whether it's pre- or post-pub cooking, these are great ways to ensure you're not missing out on a decent meal. There are ideas for the times when you're keen to pick up something Fresh from Today on the way home from work, as well as options for a Larder Loot if you haven't made it to the shops and are keen on clearing out your cupboards. These dishes are a race against the clock – but one you'll always win.

BREAKFAST
Fancy Fruit Salad: Feta, Watermelon, Berries, Beetroot & Mint (v)
No time to spare, but getting in the good stuff.

LUNCH
Chirashi Sushi Bowl
Carrying on the healthy and wholesome theme.

SNACK
Asparagus, Parmesan & Pesto Crostini (v)
You're having a late dinner, and a substantial snack is needed.

FRESHFROMTODAY

DINNER
Tagliata with Crispy Oyster Mushrooms,
Rosemary & Parmesan
It's been a long week, so go all out on dinner – you deserve it.

DESSERT
Blood Orange, Black Pepper & Basil Granita (v)
You're in need of something sweet and refreshing to finish the day on.

LEFTOVERS
Rare Beef & Pomegranate Salad

(v) = vegetarian option

Preparation time: 10 minutes | **Feeds:** 4–6

FANCY FRUIT SALAD: FETA, WATERMELON, BERRIES, BEETROOT & MINT

This is the perfect summer combination. It doesn't only work as a breakfast dish but is also great as a refreshing side dish for barbecues and red meat.

220 g (7¾ oz) feta
5 generous slices of watermelon,
   cut into rough chunks
2 handfuls of blueberries
2 handfuls of blackberries
handful of mint leaves, shredded
generous drizzle of honey
4 cooked beetroot (beets),
   cut into small wedges
thick Greek-style yogurt and ground
   cinnamon, to serve – optional

Crumble the feta into a large serving bowl, then add the watermelon, berries, mint and honey. Mix well, so the honey coats everything.

Spoon into individual serving bowls, then add the beetroot (this keeps it from looking messy and stops everything getting covered in beetroot juice). If you like, add a dollop of yogurt and a light dusting of cinnamon.

Preparation time: 30 minutes | **Cooking time:** 30 minutes | **Feeds:** 6

CHIRASHI
SUSHI BOWL

The trick with this is to prepare the rice in advance. Although it's traditionally made with raw fish, pickles, fresh vegetables and herbs, don't be afraid to mix it up. Other great toppings include finely shredded carrot, mushrooms, sautéed onion, salmon roe, cooked spinach, hard-boiled eggs and bamboo shoots, but really the options are endless. Just use your favourite fish and veg and you're good to go. Here's mine.

500 g (1 lb 2 oz/2¼ cups) sushi rice

115 ml (3¾ fl oz/scant ½ cup) sushi vinegar

300 g (10½ oz) sashimi-grade salmon, cut into thin strips

4 tablespoons soy sauce, plus extra to serve

1 tablespoon rice wine vinegar

1 tablespoon caster (superfine) sugar

½ teaspoon wasabi paste, plus extra to serve

1 hass avocado

4 large radishes, thinly sliced

4 hard-boiled eggs, peeled and sliced

1 spring onion (scallion), thinly sliced

2 tablespoons pickled ginger, drained

3 sheets nori seaweed, cut into fine strips, plus extra to serve

4 crab sticks, shredded – optional

bunch of coriander (cilantro), leaves picked

Start by thoroughly rinsing the rice in cold water. Place the rice in a rice cooker or saucepan, then cover with 580 ml (20¼ fl oz/2⅓ cups) of water and leave the rice to soak for 30 minutes. Either turn on the rice cooker or place the pan over high heat and bring to the boil, then turn down the heat as low as possible, cover with a tight-fitting lid and cook for 12–15 minutes or until all the water has been absorbed. Remove from the heat and leave to stand, still covered, for 10 minutes. Add the sushi vinegar to the warm rice and mix together thoroughly.

Lay the salmon strips on a plate. Combine the soy sauce, rice wine vinegar, sugar and wasabi and pour over the salmon, then cover with plastic wrap and leave to marinate for 5–10 minutes.

When you're almost ready to serve, slice the avocado and arrange on a platter, along with the radishes, drained salmon, eggs, spring onion, ginger, nori and crab sticks, if using. Place small bowls of coriander leaves, plus extra soy sauce, wasabi and nori on the table.

Spoon the rice into individual serving bowls and let people help themselves to the toppings.

TIP If you can't find sushi vinegar, make your own by combining 60 ml (2 fl oz/¼ cup) rice vinegar with 2 tablespoons sugar and ½ teaspoon salt. Heat gently, stirring to dissolve the sugar, then leave to cool.

Preparation time: 10 minutes | **Feeds:** 4–6

ASPARAGUS, PARMESAN & PESTO CROSTINI

For me this seasonal treat can't be beaten. The uncooked asparagus adds a fresh crispness to the crostini, while the peppery pesto gives it a bit of a kick. To save time on the day, make the pesto in advance and store in an airtight jar for up to two days in the fridge. Anything goes with pesto!

200 g (7 oz) asparagus
glug of extra virgin olive oil
1 loaf of sourdough
2 large cloves garlic, cut in half
   lengthways
70 g (2½ oz) parmesan, shaved

PESTO
½ clove garlic
1 large handful of finely grated
   parmesan
1 smaller handful of pine nuts
2 large handfuls of basil leaves,
   roughly chopped
juice of ½ lemon, to taste
2 generous glugs of extra virgin
   olive oil

For the pesto, use a pestle and mortar to pound the garlic to a paste with a pinch of salt and a generous amount of black pepper. Add the parmesan and pine nuts and pound until you have a thick paste. Gradually add the basil leaves and keep pounding until you have a thick green paste. Stir in the lemon juice and olive oil, then taste and add more lemon juice or olive oil if you think it needs it.

Shave the asparagus into ribbons using a mandoline or vegetable peeler, then place in a large bowl. Add a glug of olive oil and a dollop of pesto and gently toss together.

Slice and toast the sourdough, then rub one side of each slice with the cut surface of the garlic cloves.

Place a small mound of asparagus on each crostini, then top with parmesan shavings and an extra dollop of pesto. Serve immediately.

Preparation time: 5 minutes | **Cooking time:** 10 minutes | **Feeds:** 4–6 (or 2 with leftovers)

TAGLIATA WITH CRISPY OYSTER MUSHROOMS, ROSEMARY & PARMESAN

I know I've said this a few times now, but this is actually another favourite dish. What could be better than a steak cooked to perfection and served rare? This Italian way with steak is delicious and, at the end of the working week, who doesn't deserve a treat?

2 sirloin steaks (about 600 g/1 lb 5 oz in total) – the best quality you can afford

2 glugs of extra virgin olive oil

8 oyster mushrooms, torn into large pieces

4 cloves garlic, crushed

3 sprigs of rosemary

40 g (1½ oz) parmesan, shaved

2 large handfuls of rocket (arugula)

Season the steaks with salt and pepper, then place a skillet or heavy-based frying pan over high heat. Add a dash of olive oil and wait until it starts to smoke, then add the steaks. Cook for 2–2½ minutes (depending on their thickness), turning them every 10 seconds. Transfer the cooked steaks to a wire rack to rest for at least 5 minutes, placing a plate underneath to catch all the juices.

Meanwhile, add the oyster mushrooms to the same pan, with a little more oil if needed, then turn the heat up to high and let them brown for a minute or so on both sides. Add the garlic, rosemary and a sprinkling of salt and pepper, then pour in any juices that have drained from the steaks and cook for a minute or so.

To serve, slice the steaks thinly on the diagonal and arrange on a board or platter. Place the parmesan and rocket in separate bowls and dress the rocket with a generous drizzle of olive oil. Put the mushrooms onto a serving plate, pouring any pan juices into a jug.

BLOOD ORANGE, BLACK PEPPER & BASIL GRANITA

Super-easy to make, this granita is seriously refreshing. And I love the idea of turning dessert into an after-dinner digestif.

2 tablespoons caster (superfine) sugar
300 ml (10½ fl oz) boiling water
handful of basil leaves
2 blood oranges, peeled
1 litre (35 fl oz/4 cups) blood orange juice
200 ml (7 fl oz) lemon juice

Dissolve the sugar in the boiling water.

Using a pestle and mortar, pound the basil leaves to a paste.

Put the sugar syrup, blood oranges, blood orange juice, lemon juice and ½ teaspoon of freshly ground black pepper in a blender and briefly blitz to break up the blood orange, then mix in the basil paste. Taste for seasoning and sweetness and adjust if necessary.

Transfer to a large stainless-steel tray or bowl and place in the freezer. Leave for half an hour, then scrape with a fork and return to the freezer for another half hour. Scrape again, then freeze for another half hour, by which time it should be properly frozen. Scrape again before serving.

TIP If you're barely home, just combine the ingredients listed with 4 scoops of ice in a blender and serve immediately. Or add 6 shots of tequila to turn this into a margarita-style drink and really get the party started.

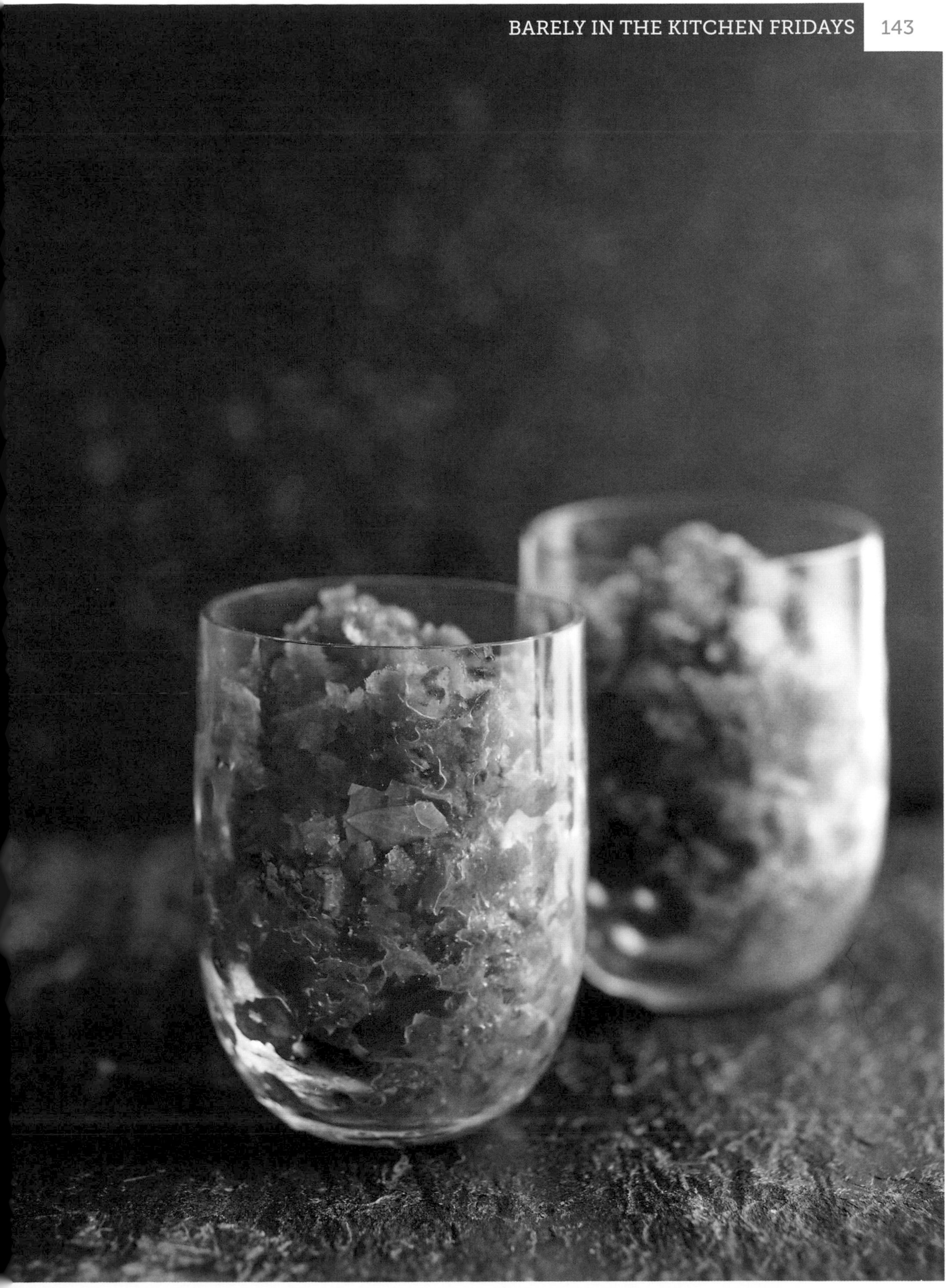

RARE BEEF & POMEGRANATE SALAD

This dish is fragrant, light and quick to make. If you like steak, spice and bold flavours, this is the dish for you.

about 250 g (9 oz) left-over tagliata (see page 141) or sirloin steak
small glug of sesame oil
½ red onion, thinly sliced
½ red chilli, thinly sliced
3 cm (1¼ in) knob of ginger, finely shredded
seeds from ½ pomegranate
3 pickled beetroot (beets), drained and cut into quarters
2 tablespoons chopped coriander (cilantro)
2 tablespoons mint leaves
2 tablespoons Thai basil leaves

DRESSING
2 tablespoons rice wine vinegar
1 tablespoon light soy sauce
2 teaspoons fish sauce
½ teaspoon palm sugar or caster (superfine) sugar
juice of ½ lime

If starting from scratch rather than using left-over tagliata, season the steak with salt and white pepper. Heat the sesame oil in a skillet or heavy-based frying pan over high heat until it starts to smoke. Add the steak and cook for 2–2½ minutes (depending on its thickness), turning it every 10 seconds. Transfer the cooked steak to a wire rack to cool, placing a plate underneath to catch all the juices.

Meanwhile, make the dressing. Combine all the ingredients in a small bowl and stir until the palm sugar dissolves. Have a taste – you're aiming for a tangy but sweet flavour, so adjust accordingly until you're happy.

In a large bowl, gently toss together the onion, chilli, ginger, pomegranate seeds, beetroot, coriander, mint and Thai basil.

When the steak is completely cool, slice it into thin strips and add to the bowl, then pour over the dressing. Leave to marinate for a few minutes before serving.

BREAKFAST
Coffee & Banana Breakfast Smoothie
Your cupboards are running low... work with what you've got.

LUNCH
Any Veg Broth with Parsley Pesto (v)
Having a bit of a clear out.

SNACK
Radishes with Black Olive Tapenade (v)
Using up the jars and tins.

LARDERLOOT

DINNER
Pub Peanut Noodle Salad (v)
Really using up those last bits of veg, plus peanuts from the pub – this needs to be quick and have spice.

DESSERT
Espresso Martini Affogato (v)
In need of a little pick-me-up post dinner and after a long week?

LEFTOVERS
Crispy Noodle Bundles with Sweet Chilli Dip (v)

(v) = vegetarian option

Preparation time: 5 minutes | **Feeds:** 2

COFFEE & BANANA
BREAKFAST SMOOTHIE

If there's one meal of the day you shouldn't miss, it's breakfast. With a smoothie this quick and easy to make and drink, there's no excuse. And coffee and banana do two jobs in one!

double shot of espresso, left to cool
2 ripe bananas, cut into chunks
    and frozen
260 g (9¼ oz/1 cup) plain yogurt,
    frozen yogurt or ice-cream
1 tablespoon cocoa powder
¼ teaspoon ground cinnamon
250 ml (9 fl oz/1 cup) coconut milk,
    almond milk or regular milk

Place all the ingredients except the milk in a blender. With the motor running, gradually add the milk and blitz until smooth. Pour into two glasses and drink straightaway.

TIP Almond milk is a healthy alternative, and makes a great smoothie.

Preparation time: 10 minutes | **Cooking time:** 20 minutes | **Feeds:** 4

ANY VEG BROTH
WITH PARSLEY PESTO

This is where you get to choose whether to be creative or just use up what you have left over. I'm a huge fan of a light broth, and this parsley pesto makes sure you're not short of flavour.

glug of rapeseed oil

1 white onion, diced

2 cloves garlic, thinly sliced

1 carrot, diced

½ leek, diced

½ head of broccoli, broken into florets
    and roughly chopped

1 x 400 g (14 oz) tin of butter beans —
    or whatever beans you have

1 bay leaf

3 sprigs of fresh thyme or ½ teaspoon
    dried thyme

1.5 litres (52 fl oz/6 cups) vegetable
    stock

2 tablespoons yogurt, crème fraîche
    or sour cream

PARSLEY PESTO

1 clove garlic

1 tablespoon pine nuts

large handful of finely chopped
    parsley

25 g (1 oz/¼ cup) finely grated
    parmesan

big glug of extra virgin olive oil

Pour the rapeseed oil into a large saucepan, add the onion, garlic, carrot, leek and broccoli and sweat over medium–low heat for a few minutes until starting to soften. Add the butter beans, bay leaf and thyme. Season with salt and pepper, pour in the vegetable stock and bring to the boil. Reduce the heat and simmer for 12–15 minutes until the vegetables are tender.

For the parsley pesto, pound the garlic, pine nuts and parsley to a paste using a pestle and mortar (or whiz them in a small food processor or blender). Season to taste with salt and pepper, then stir in the parmesan and olive oil. Add a spoonful of pesto to each bowl of soup, along with a dollop of yogurt, crème fraîche or sour cream.

TIP You can really use up any left-over veg you have: courgette (zucchini), kale, green beans, spinach, mushrooms, celery, mange tout (snow peas), cauliflower, fresh or frozen peas... Just cut everything into small, similar-sized pieces, so it cooks quickly and evenly.

RADISHES WITH BLACK OLIVE TAPENADE

This is the perfect balance of big flavours. Just make sure you use a hot radish: organic ones usually have more kick to them, as do the long black Spanish variety. The crispness of the radishes contrasted with the intense saltiness of the olives and anchovies is so good. Once you start munching on these, you won't stop.

10–15 radishes, any larger ones
    cut in half

BLACK OLIVE TAPENADE
1 clove garlic, finely chopped
4 tablespoons capers
3 anchovy fillets, chopped
250 g (9 oz) Greek-style dry-cured
    olives, pitted
small handful of roughly chopped
    parsley
3 tablespoons extra virgin olive oil
squeeze of lemon juice

Using a mortar and pestle, pound all the tapenade ingredients with a grinding of pepper to a coarse, rustic paste (or keep pounding until smooth if you prefer it that way). Taste for seasoning and adjust if necessary.

Mix the tapenade through the radishes, then let people help themselves.

Preparation time: 30 minutes | **Feeds:** 6 (or 2 with leftovers)

PUB PEANUT
NOODLE SALAD

The aim of this dish is to use up all the left-over bits you have in the fridge.
I'm always mindful to not use everything in the fridge during the week,
so I can make something like this with leftovers most weeks. That way,
this ends up costing next to nothing to make... it's a freebie!

200 g dried rice vermicelli

1 x 400 g (14 oz) tin of kidney beans,
   rinsed and drained

1 spring onion (scallion), thinly sliced

¼ red cabbage, finely shredded

½ courgette (zucchini), shaved into
   ribbons using a vegetable peeler

1 roasted red pepper (capsicum) –
   the jarred ones are great for this

70 g (2½ oz/½ cup) frozen peas

DRESSING

3 cloves garlic, peeled

1 red chilli, roughly chopped

2 tablespoons palm sugar or
   caster (superfine) sugar

2 generous glugs of rice wine vinegar

2 tablespoons fish sauce – leave out
   for a vegetarian version

GARNISHES

3 hard-boiled eggs, cut into quarters

handful of peanuts from the pub
   (or shop), ground

2 limes, cut into quarters

2 red chillies, thinly sliced

handful of chopped coriander
   (cilantro)

For the dressing, pound all the ingredients together using a pestle and mortar, then season with white pepper.

Put the rice vermicelli into a heatproof bowl, cover with boiling water and leave for 10–15 minutes until soft, then drain. Rinse under cold running water and drain again.

Combine all the ingredients except the garnishes in a large serving dish. Check that the seasoning is just right, then pour over the dressing and mix to coat everything evenly.

Garnish with the eggs, peanuts, limes, chillies and coriander, then serve immediately.

ESPRESSO MARTINI
AFFOGATO

This is a cheat's dessert and digestif in one... with minimum effort required, it's perfect if you're short of time.

4 shots good-quality vodka

4 shots Kahlua or other coffee-flavoured liqueur

8 shots espresso

4 generous scoops good-quality vanilla ice cream

50 g (1¾ oz) dark chocolate, coarsely grated

Combine the vodka, Kahlua and espresso in a small saucepan and warm through for a minute – no longer, otherwise you'll start cooking off the alcohol.

Place a scoop of vanilla ice cream in each serving dish, then pour over the vodka, Kahlua and coffee mixture and sprinkle over the grated chocolate.

Eat straightaway, before it melts!

CRISPY NOODLE BUNDLES
WITH SWEET CHILLI DIP

These flavoursome little bundles offer contrasting textures and fresh zesty flavours, especially if you're using up left-over noodle salad. I'm a sucker for a sweet chilli dip. In fact, sweet chilli anything is a winner.

2 big spoonfuls of left-over pub peanut noodle salad (see page 155)
150–200 g (5½–7 oz) cooked egg noodles, depending on how much left-over noodle salad you have
drizzle of sesame oil
1 tablespoon black sesame seeds
glug of soy sauce
2 eggs, lightly beaten
150 g (5½ oz/1 cup) plain (all-purpose) flour
rapeseed oil for deep-frying

SWEET CHILLI DIP
220 g (7¾ oz/1 cup) caster (superfine) sugar
125 ml (4 fl oz/½ cup) rice wine vinegar
2 red chillies, chopped – remove the seeds if you want a milder sauce
3 cloves garlic, thinly sliced
2 teaspoons cornflour (cornstarch), mixed with a splash of water

Start by making the sweet chilli dip. Combine the sugar, rice wine vinegar, chillies and garlic with 250 ml (9 fl oz/1 cup) of water in a saucepan. Bring to the boil and cook for 10 minutes, then reduce the heat to low and stir in the cornflour mixture. Remove from the heat and leave to cool for a few minutes. Either leave as is for a rustic, homemade effect, or blitz with a stick blender or in a food processor until smooth.

Place the left-over noodle salad and the egg noodles in a large bowl. Add the sesame oil, sesame seeds, soy sauce, a sprinkle of white pepper and the beaten eggs, then mix thoroughly.

Put the flour in a shallow bowl and season with salt and black pepper. Then use a fork to twirl the noodles into little bundles. Gently slip the bundles off the fork and into the flour, carefully coat each side with flour, set to one side until you've used up all the noodle mixture.

Pour a 3–4 cm (1¼–1½ in) depth of oil into a large frying pan or wok and heat to 180°C (350°F). If you don't have a thermometer, check that it's hot enough by dropping a piece of noodle in – it should immediately sizzle and float to the top. Working in small batches, cook the noodle bundles in the hot oil for 2–3 minutes or until crisp and golden all over, then remove with tongs or a slotted spoon and drain on paper towel.

Serve with the sweet chilli dip for dunking.

TIP Keep the crispy noodle bundles warm in a 150°C (300°F/gas mark 2) oven while you cook the rest.

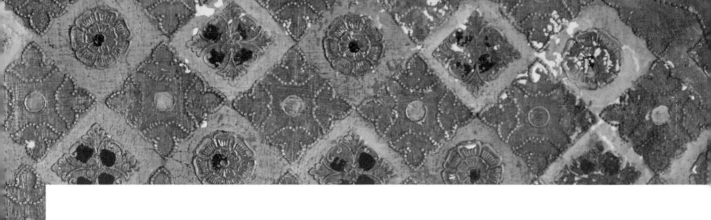

SOMETHING
SPECIAL
SATURDAYS

By the time Saturday comes around, I'm always ready to whip up something a bit different. This is about going all out. You've got the option to stay On a Budget or blow it by Splashing the Cash; either way, the options are pretty special, ensuring you'll impress yourself and everyone else. It's good to indulge!

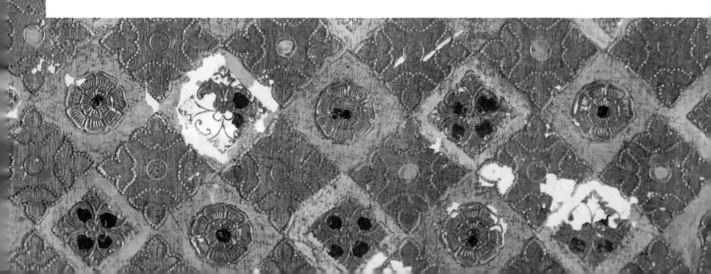

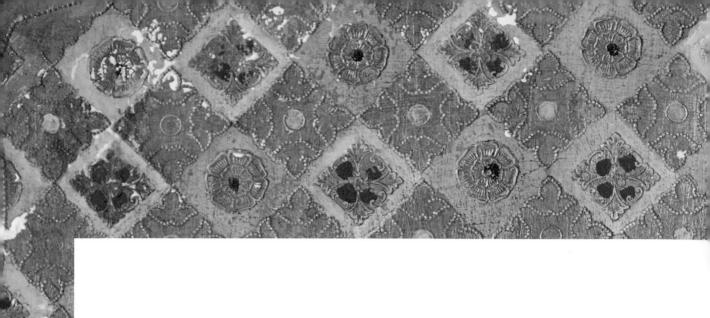

BREAKFAST
Kimchi Pancake (v)
Watching the pennies, but in need of something exciting?

LUNCH
Pineapple Papaya Salad (v)
Sticking with spice.

SNACK
Dumplings with Crunch... Three Ways (v)
Got a bit of time and up for some cooking?

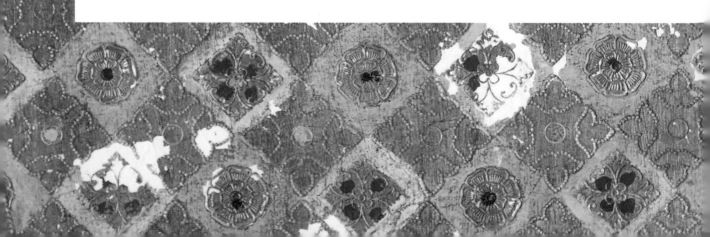

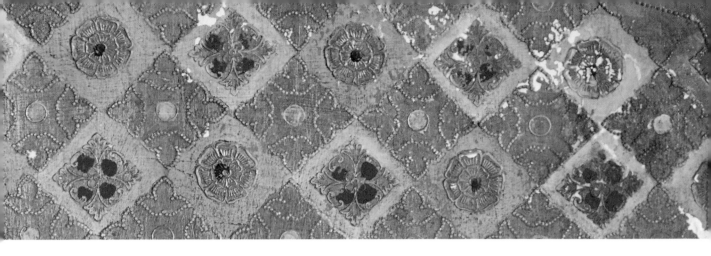

ONABUDGET

DINNER
Cheat's Aubergine Parmigiana (v)
No need for meat today, just something hearty to end on.

DESSERT
Peanut Butter & Cherry Chocolate Cups (v)
Can't resist a little something sweet?

LEFTOVERS
Moussaka My Way

(v) = vegetarian option

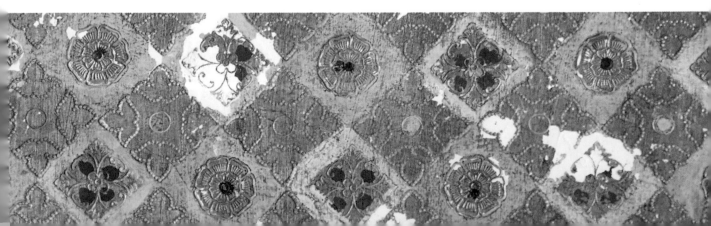

Preparation time: 10 minutes | **Cooking time:** 10 minutes | **Feeds:** 4

KIMCHI PANCAKE

This is one of my favourite Korean dishes. It's so easy to make and packed full of flavour – a definite wake-me-up.

150 g (5½ oz) kimchi, drained –
  but keep the liquid
100 g (3½ oz/⅔ cup) plain
  (all-purpose) flour
3 free-range eggs, lightly beaten
2 spring onions (scallions),
  thinly sliced
1 clove garlic, finely chopped or grated
generous glug of vegetable oil

DIPPING SAUCE
2 large glugs of light soy sauce
2 tablespoons rice wine vinegar
2 teaspoons sesame oil
½ red chilli, thinly sliced

Squeeze the kimchi dry with your hands, then roughly chop. In a bowl, combine the kimchi with 125 ml (4 fl oz/½ cup) of its liquid, the flour, eggs, spring onions and garlic.

Heat the vegetable oil in a large non-stick frying pan over a medium heat, then add the pancake mixture and cook for around 2–3 minutes or until crisp and golden brown. Carefully slide the pancake onto a plate, then gently flip it back into the pan and cook on the other side for 2–3 minutes.

Meanwhile, for the dipping sauce, simply mix all the ingredients together and you're ready to dunk.

Cut the pancake into quarters and serve with the dipping sauce on the side.

TIP For a bit more kick, top with extra kimchi and red chilli, then garnish with coriander (cilantro) leaves and sliced spring onion (scallion).

Preparation time: 20 minutes | **Feeds:** 4–6 (or more as a side dish)

PINEAPPLE PAPAYA SALAD

There's nothing I don't love about this salad. You can buy the frozen papaya at most Asian supermarkets – it's cheaper and much quicker than shredding fresh green papaya.

1 x 500 g (1 lb 2 oz) pack of frozen shredded green papaya, defrosted and drained
½ red onion, thinly sliced
1 carrot, thinly sliced lengthways
¼ fresh pineapple or 2–3 rings of tinned pineapple, cut into 2 cm (¾ in) chunks
4 sprigs of mint, leaves picked
handful of coriander (cilantro), roughly chopped
juice of 1 lime
½ red chilli, thinly sliced
handful of peanuts, coarsely crushed

DRESSING
3 cloves garlic
2 red chillies, chopped – remove the seeds for a less fiery dressing
2 tablespoons palm sugar or caster (superfine) sugar
6 cherry tomatoes
4 large glugs of rice wine vinegar
2 tablespoons fish sauce – leave this out if cooking for vegetarians

For the dressing, pound all the ingredients using a pestle and mortar, starting with the garlic, chillies, palm sugar and a sprinkle of salt. Add the cherry tomatoes and pound lightly (use your hand as a cover, or you'll end up splattered with tomato seeds). You don't want this too fine – pound just enough so there are no huge lumps of garlic, palm sugar or tomato. Stir in the vinegar, fish sauce and a dash of white pepper and have a try: it should be equally sweet and sour.

Place the papaya, onion, carrot and pineapple in a bowl. Pour over the dressing and stir well, then chill in the fridge for around 10 minutes to let the dressing infuse the papaya.

Gently stir the mint, coriander and lime juice into the salad, then garnish with chilli slices and a sprinkling of crushed peanuts.

Preparation time: 25 minutes | **Cooking time:** 20 minutes | **Feeds:** 4–6

DUMPLINGS WITH CRUNCH...
THREE WAYS

The half-fried, half-steamed dumpling is the most superior of dumplings. Don't be afraid to give these a go – you won't regret it. Remember to leave out the fish sauce (and choose the mushroom filling) if cooking for vegetarians!

1 large banana shallot, finely diced

2 cloves garlic, crushed

5 cm (2 in) knob of ginger, finely grated

½ red chilli, finely diced

½ carrot, finely diced

1 tablespoon finely chopped chives

1 tablespoon finely chopped coriander (cilantro)

2 tablespoons light soy sauce

1 tablespoon of fish sauce – optional

about 40 wonton wrappers

generous glug of rapeseed oil

PLUS YOUR CHOICE OF FILLING:

1½ portobello mushrooms, finely diced

60 g (2¼ oz) minced (ground) pork

60 g (2¼ oz) peeled prawns, finely diced

DIPPING SAUCE

1 tablespoon finely chopped coriander (cilantro)

½ spring onion (scallion), thinly sliced

¼ red chilli, finely chopped

1 teaspoon palm sugar or caster (superfine) sugar

3 tablespoons light soy sauce

3 tablespoons rice wine vinegar

2 teaspoons fish sauce – optional

In a bowl, combine the shallot, garlic, ginger, chilli, carrot, herbs, soy sauce and fish sauce (if using) and mix thoroughly. Add your choice of filling, season with salt and pepper and mix thoroughly again.

Take a wonton paper and put a teaspoon of the mixture in the centre. Using either your finger or a pastry brush, wet the edges of the wonton paper with warm water, then fold into a triangle to enclose the mixture before sticking the sides down. Press the edges together to seal, ensuring there's no air trapped inside the dumpling (or they may burst on cooking). Repeat until all the filling has been used up.

Pour a good glug of rapeseed oil into your largest frying pan and place over medium heat. When the oil is hot, add the dumplings and cook for 2–3 minutes or until the base of the dumplings is golden and crispy. Add a dash of water, then cover with a lid or foil and steam the dumplings for 2–4 minutes or until they are soft and cooked through – the water should have completely evaporated by this point.

For the dipping sauce, combine all the ingredients in a small serving bowl.

Serve the dumplings straightaway with the dipping sauce.

TIP When making dumplings, it's a good idea to cook a test one first, then taste it to make sure you have the seasoning right.

Preparation time: 30 minutes | **Cooking time:** 40 minutes–1½ hours | **Feeds:** 6–8 (or 4 with leftovers)

CHEAT'S AUBERGINE
PARMIGIANA

I'm always torn between spicy foods and hearty Italian dishes – this is for when I'm in the mood for the latter. Make sure you put some time in with your sauce and you won't go wrong, even though this dish cuts corners and requires a lot less effort than the traditional method.

4 aubergines (eggplants), sliced into
    rounds about 1 cm (½ in) thick
olive oil
1 white onion, finely diced
1 carrot, finely diced
3 large cloves garlic, roughly chopped
1 tablespoon dried oregano
170 ml (5½ fl oz/⅔ cup) white wine
2 x 400 g (14 oz) tins of chopped
    tomatoes
250 ml (9 fl oz/1 cup) vegetable stock
3 x 125 g (4½ oz) balls of mozzarella
3–4 slices of sourdough or rustic
    white bread
large handful of basil leaves,
    roughly chopped
handful of parsley leaves,
    roughly chopped
70 g (2½ oz/⅔ cup) finely grated
    parmesan

Preheat the oven to 200°C (400°F/gas mark 6). Place the aubergine slices in a single layer on generously oiled non-stick baking trays and season with salt and pepper. Roast for 20–25 minutes or until the aubergine begins to soften.

Meanwhile, get started on your tomato sauce. Pour a big glug of oil into a large pan and add the onion, carrot, garlic and oregano, along with a sprinkle of salt and pepper. Cook over medium heat for 4–5 minutes or until the onion is translucent, then add the white wine, tomatoes and stock and bring to the boil. Let it bubble for 5 minutes before turning the heat down to medium–low and leaving the sauce to simmer for at least 20 minutes; if you have time, let it cook for 40 minutes–1 hour.

Next prepare the mozzarella and breadcrumbs: chop or tear both the cheese and bread into roughly 1 cm (½ in) cubes.

When the tomato sauce is done, add half of the basil and parsley and check the seasoning. Remove the aubergines from the oven and reduce the temperature to 190°C (375°F/gas mark 5). You're now ready to start building the dish.

Place a layer of aubergine in a deep baking dish or tin. Add a layer of tomato sauce and a sprinkling of basil and parsley, followed by a few pieces of mozzarella and some roughly torn breadcrumbs. Repeat these layers until you've used everything up – you're aiming for around four layers in total. Make sure you save enough breadcrumbs to combine with the grated parmesan for the final layer.

Bake for 15–20 minutes or until golden and crispy on the top. Serve straightaway.

Preparation time: 10 minutes | **Chilling time:** at least 1 hour | **Makes:** 10

PEANUT BUTTER & CHERRY CHOCOLATE CUPS

If you're addicted to Reese's Peanut Butter Cups, here's how to make an even better version at home. To really glam these up, decorate them with cherries gilded with edible gold spray, which is available from specialist food shops.

150 g (5½ oz) milk chocolate
150 g (5½ oz) dark chocolate
150 ml (5 fl oz) double (thick) cream
300 g (10½ oz) crunchy peanut butter
100 g (3½ oz) glacé cherries, finely chopped
150 g (5½ oz) fresh cherries
handful of mixed nuts or granola
10 paper cupcake cases

Break all the chocolate into small chunks, then melt in a heatproof bowl set over a pan of simmering water (make sure the base of the bowl isn't touching the water).

In a separate pan, heat the cream until it is warm to the touch (don't let it come to the boil), then whisk into the melted chocolate until you have a smooth thick sauce. Add 2 tablespoons of peanut butter to the chocolate mixture, whisking until it dissolves, then stir in the glacé cherries.

Spread out your cupcake cases on a tray or large plate and place ½ teaspoon of peanut butter in each one.

Spoon or pipe in the chocolate mixture, dividing it evenly between the cases, then decorate with fresh cherries and mixed nuts or granola. Chill for 1 hour in the freezer or several hours in the fridge.

TIP If you have a muffin tin, sit the cupcake cases in it before filling them, so they keep their shape as the chocolate mixture cools and firms.

Preparation time: 10 minutes | **Cooking time:** 1 hour | **Feeds:** 4–6

MOUSSAKA MY WAY

Moussaka is one of those comforting dishes I can easily eat a pile of, plus there's the added bonus of a crispy cheese topping! For a vegetarian moussaka, just leave out the lamb.

about 1 large serving of left-over
  aubergine parmigiana (see page
  171) or 1 large aubergine (eggplant),
  sliced into 1 cm (½ in) rounds
1 red onion, cut into rings
1 courgette (zucchini), sliced
  into 1 cm (½ in) rounds
600 g (1 lb 5 oz) potatoes,
  peeled and sliced
big glug of rapeseed oil

LAMB & LENTIL SAUCE
glug of olive oil
½ red onion, diced
3 cloves garlic, thinly sliced
500 g (1 lb 2 oz) minced (ground) lamb
1 x 400 g (14 oz) tin of tomatoes
big glug of red wine
4 tablespoons dried red lentils
2 teaspoons dried oregano
sprinkle of sugar
1 tablespoon chopped parsley

CHEESE SAUCE
40 g (1½ oz) butter, melted
1 teaspoon dijon mustard
3 tablespoons plain (all-purpose) flour
400 ml (14 fl oz) semi-skimmed milk
75 g (2½ oz/¾ cup) grated mature
  cheddar
25 g (1 oz/¼ cup) finely grated parmesan

Preheat the oven to 190°C (375°F/gas mark 5).

Put the left-over parmigiana or aubergine in a large roasting tin, then add the onion, courgette and potatoes. Drizzle everything generously with rapeseed oil and sprinkle with salt, then roast for 15–20 minutes or until all the vegetables are tender and golden.

Meanwhile, for the lamb and lentil sauce, pour a glug of olive oil into a saucepan over medium heat. Add the onion and garlic and cook for 2 minutes or until the onion softens. Add the lamb and cook over high heat until it browns, then add the tomatoes, red wine, lentils and oregano. Season with the sugar, salt and pepper and cook for 10–20 minutes or until the sauce is richly flavoured and the meat and lentils are cooked through. Finally, stir in the parsley.

For the cheese sauce, melt the butter in a saucepan over medium–low heat, then whisk in the mustard and flour until it forms a paste. Season with salt and pepper, then gradually add the milk, whisking constantly, until you have a thick, smooth sauce. Add three-quarters of the cheddar and stir until it has melted into the sauce.

Place a layer of the lamb and lentil sauce in a large baking dish, followed by a layer of roast vegetables, then a drizzle of cheese sauce. Repeat these layers until all the ingredients are used up, making sure you save enough cheese sauce to cover the top. Combine the remaining cheddar with the parmesan and sprinkle over the top, then bake in the oven for 15–20 minutes or until crisp and golden.

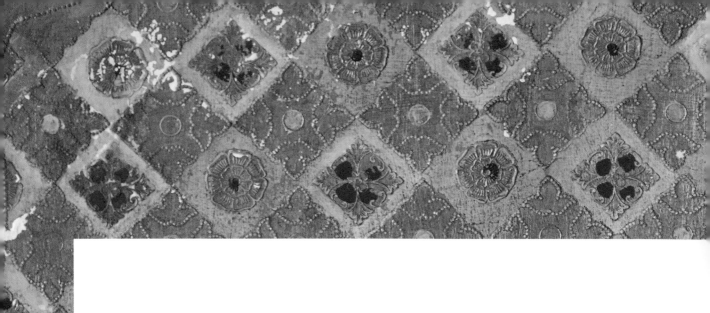

BREAKFAST
Smoked Salmon, Spinach & Ricotta Frittata
Fancy indulging?

LUNCH
Stuffed Meatball Baps with French Dip
Up for taking a trip to the local butchers and going all out?

SNACK
Orange, Fennel, Rocket & Roasties (v)
Fancy something zesty and fresh?

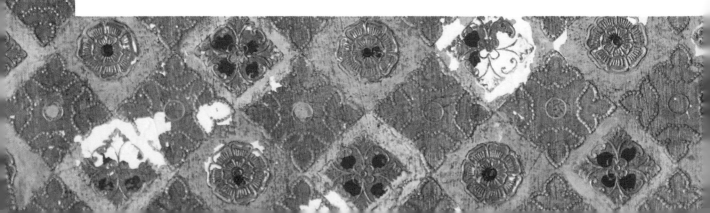

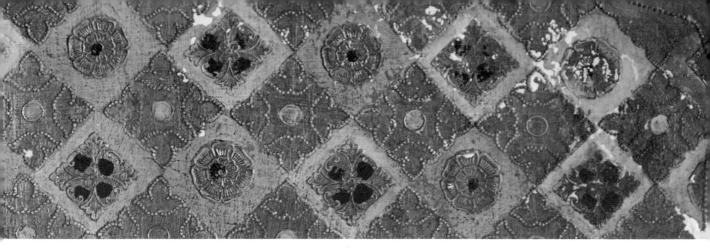

SPLASHTHECASH

DINNER
Squid Ink Pasta Ribbons with King Prawns & Star Anise
*Got some time on your hands and ready to get down
to some home cooking?*

DESSERT
Crème Pâtissière Chocolate Profiteroles (v)
Not one to leave yourself or others hungry?

LEFTOVERS
Spinach & Leek Squid Ink Pasta Bake

(v) = vegetarian option

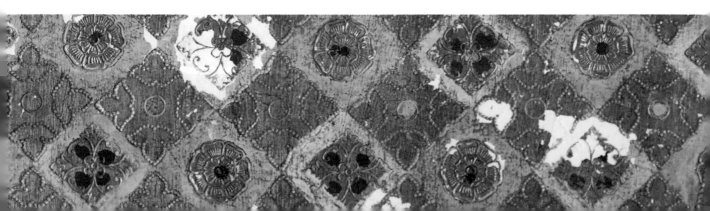

Preparation time: 15 minutes | **Cooking time:** 20 minutes | **Feeds:** 4–6

SMOKED SALMON, SPINACH & RICOTTA FRITTATA

If you've got guests, this is the perfect breakfast dish – just get everything in the one large pan and cook. What could be easier? This is packed full of flavour, light and fresh.

300 g (10½ oz) spinach leaves, thoroughly washed
glug of olive oil
knob of butter
1 white onion, roughly chopped
4 tablespoons capers
220 g (7¾ oz) ricotta
½ teaspoon freshly grated nutmeg
finely grated zest of ½ lemon
6 large free-range eggs
glug of milk
3 large dollops of crème fraîche (sour cream)
300 g (10½ oz) sustainable smoked salmon, cut into strips
50 g (1¾ oz) parmesan, shaved
lamb's lettuce, capers – and fancy caviar, if you're really blowing the budget – to garnish

Start by wilting your spinach in a pan over medium–low heat, then drain in a sieve, pressing out as much liquid as possible, and set aside.

Place a non-stick frying pan over medium heat and add the oil and butter. When the butter has melted, add the onion, capers, ricotta, nutmeg and lemon zest and stir until warmed through. Spread the ricotta mixture evenly over the base of the pan and add the spinach.

Whisk together the eggs and milk, season with salt and pepper, then pour into the pan. Dot with dollops of crème fraîche and cook over medium heat for 4–5 minutes. Sprinkle over half of the smoked salmon and half of the parmesan, then cook under the grill (broiler) for 2–3 minutes until golden. Be careful to not overcook the frittata; slightly sloppy is a good thing in this case.

Garnish with the lamb's lettuce, capers and the remaining smoked salmon and parmesan (and the caviar, if going all out), then serve in the pan.

Preparation time: 10 minutes | **Cooking time:** 30 minutes | **Feeds:** 4

STUFFED MEATBALL BAPS
WITH FRENCH DIP

This is a monster of a dish if ever there was one. Take this on as a personal challenge or invite mates round and see who can get through it first. It's a man's meal (although I've eaten a few), and definitely a conversation starter if you go for the full-size meatball.

2 red onions, sliced into rings
glug of rapeseed oil
4 bread rolls
American-style mustard and ketchup (tomato sauce), to serve

MEATBALLS
500 g (1 lb 2 oz) minced (ground) beef
150 g (5½ oz) minced (ground) pork
2 cloves garlic, finely chopped
2 teaspoons finely chopped oregano
1 tablespoon finely chopped parsley
sprig of rosemary, leaves stripped and finely chopped
1 egg, lightly beaten
2 tablespoons breadcrumbs
40 g (1½ oz) smoked provolone
glug of rapeseed oil

FRENCH DIP
½ red onion, roughly chopped
1 carrot, roughly chopped
500 ml (17 fl oz/2 cups) beef stock
glug of red wine
glug of worcestershire sauce
1 teaspoon dijon mustard
sprinkle of finely chopped oregano

Preheat the oven to 180°C (350°F/gas mark 4).

To make the meatballs, combine the two minced meats, garlic and herbs in a mixing bowl. Season with salt and pepper, then add the egg and breadcrumbs and mould into generous-sized balls (about the size of a tennis ball is good). Divide the smoked provolone into four even portions, shaping them into small balls as best you can before pushing one into the centre of each meatball. Ensure you re-mould the meat around the cheese, so it doesn't escape during the cooking.

Pour a glug of oil into a frying pan over medium–high heat and brown the meatballs all over. Transfer to a baking dish and cook in the oven for 5–10 minutes or until the meatballs are cooked through.

For the French dip, add the onion and carrot to the same frying pan and stir to scrape up all the meaty goodness (add an extra glug of oil if it seems too dry). Cook over medium heat until the onion softens, then add the beef stock, red wine, worcestershire sauce, mustard and oregano. Season with salt and pepper, increase the heat to high and cook for 10 minutes or until it starts to thicken slightly. Have a taste and adjust the seasoning, then transfer to a serving bowl.

In a separate pan, fry the sliced red onions in a glug of oil until they soften and turn sticky.

To serve, slice the rolls in half and warm in the oven for a minute or so, then spread one half with mustard, ketchup and onions. Top with a meatball and the other half of the roll. Dunk your meatball bap in French dip, then just try and get your chops around the whole thing!

Preparation time: 10 minutes | **Cooking time:** 25 minutes | **Feeds:** 4–6

ORANGE, FENNEL, ROCKET & ROASTIES

This is the perfect summer salad, filling but fresh and a great accompaniment to any fish dish or simply served solo.

600 g (1 lb 5 oz) new potatoes, halved – or quartered, if large
large knob of butter
glug of olive oil
2 red onions, sliced into rings
2 fennel bulbs, very thinly sliced with a mandoline or sharp knife
2 large oranges, peeled and thinly sliced
2 hass avocados, sliced
250 g (9 oz) rocket (arugula)
generous glug of extra virgin olive oil
juice of 1 lemon

Put the potatoes into a pan of boiling salted water and cook for 6–7 minutes, then drain and return to the pan to dry out. Place the butter and olive oil in a large frying pan over high heat and add the potatoes, along with the onions and a sprinkle of salt. Cook until golden and cooked through, turning them regularly.

Combine the fennel, oranges, avocado and rocket in a large serving bowl. In a small jug, make a dressing by mixing the extra virgin olive oil with the lemon juice and seasoning with salt and pepper, then pour over the salad and mix thoroughly. Gently toss through the potatoes and onions, then serve immediately.

TIP If making this in advance, keep the oranges and dressing separate from the salad until ready to serve – this way your salad will stay crisp and fresh. If preparing the avocado in advance, cover with lemon juice so it doesn't go brown.

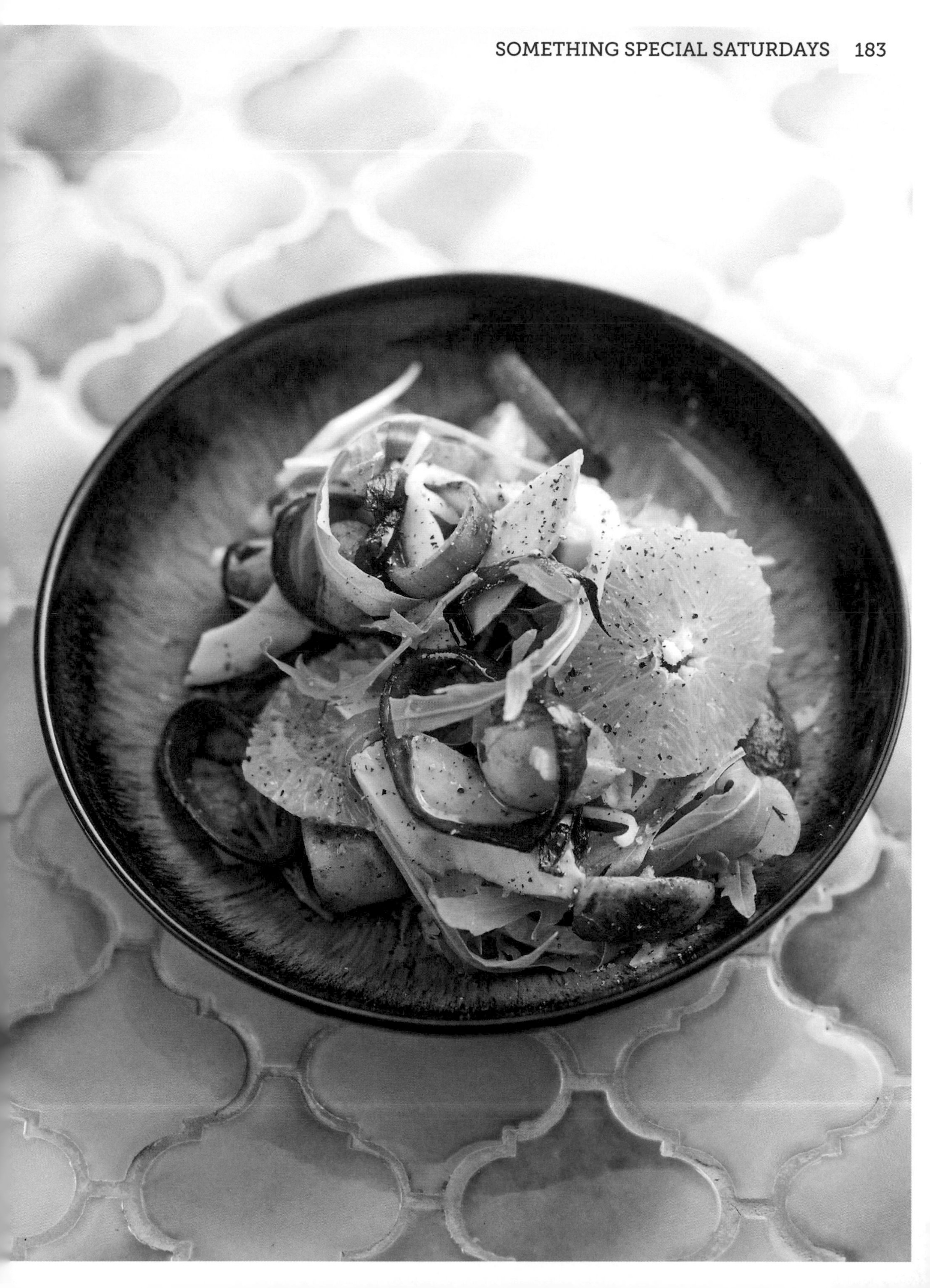

Preparation time: 1 hour (including pasta-making), plus resting time | **Cooking time:** 30 minutes
Feeds: 4 (or 2 with left-over squid ink pasta)

SQUID INK PASTA RIBBONS
WITH KING PRAWNS & STAR ANISE

I first ate this at a little vine-covered restaurant in Lindos, Rhodes, when I was 18. The chef was from the Dominican Republic, but made the most incredible Italian food, and my sister and I ate there several times a week during our stay. I made him write out the recipe, then lost it somewhere along the way. But fear not: this version is pretty much on the money.

3 generous glugs of olive oil
1 white onion, finely diced
3 large cloves garlic, finely chopped
small glug of brandy
4 star anise
small handful of chopped tarragon
   or Thai basil
250 ml (9 fl oz/1 cup) single
   (pouring) cream
300 g (10½ oz) peeled and deveined
   raw king prawns
70 g (2½ oz/⅔ cup) finely grated
   parmesan
handful of roughly chopped parsley

SQUID INK PASTA
4 x 7 g (¼ oz) sachets squid ink
4 free-range eggs
500 g (1 lb 2 oz) '00' flour
fine semolina, for sprinkling

For the pasta, beat the squid ink and eggs together with ½ teaspoon of salt. Place the flour in a mound on a clean work surface. Make a well in the middle and pour in the squid ink and eggs. Mix into the flour with a knife until it starts to come together, then knead until smooth. Wrap in plastic wrap and leave to rest at room temperature for at least 30 minutes (or up to 3 hours). Cut the dough into chunks as big as the palm of your hand and roll through each setting of a pasta machine twice. Sprinkle the pasta sheets with fine semolina, then gently fold up before slicing into ribbons: about 1 cm (½ in) is a good width.

Heat a couple of glugs of oil in a large pan over medium heat. Add the onion and garlic, season with salt and pepper and cook gently for about 5 minutes or until the onion is translucent (but don't let the garlic brown). Add the brandy and cook for 5 minutes. Next add the star anise, tarragon and cream and cook for 5 minutes. Finally, add the prawns and cook for 3 minutes.

Once the sauce is under way, cook your pasta. Fill the largest saucepan you have with boiling water, add a glug of oil and plenty of salt and bring back to the boil. Add the pasta and stir with a spoon for the first minute, so it doesn't stick. Cook over medium–high heat for 3–4 minutes or until tender, then drain.

Toss the cooked pasta and sauce together well, so every strand of pasta is coated. Serve with parmesan (I know the rules say no mixing parmesan and seafood, but...), loads of black pepper and a sprinkle of parsley.

Preparation time: 20 minutes | **Cooking time:** 50 minutes | **Feeds:** 4–6

CRÈME PÂTISSIÈRE
CHOCOLATE PROFITEROLES

My mum's the queen of profiteroles. She made hundreds for one of the pop-up restaurants we did... I've since upgraded her piping set. These are worth every minute of your time in the kitchen.

75 g (2½ oz) unsalted butter
100 g (3½ oz) plain (all-purpose) flour, sifted
3 free-range eggs, lightly beaten
finely grated chocolate, to serve

CRÈME PÂTISSIÈRE
4 egg yolks, lightly beaten
100 g (3½ oz) caster (superfine) sugar
25 g (1 oz) plain (all-purpose) flour
350 ml (12 fl oz) milk
1 vanilla pod (bean), split in half lengthways

CHOCOLATE SAUCE
100 g (3½ oz) good-quality dark chocolate
135 ml (4½ fl oz) double (thick) cream

Preheat the oven to 200°C (400°F/gas mark 6) and line a baking tray with baking paper.

Place the butter and 150 ml (5 fl oz) water in a saucepan over high heat until the butter melts and the water begins to boil. Immediately add the flour and a pinch of salt and stir vigorously with a wooden spoon until the mixture comes together. Reduce the heat to medium and keep stirring for a minute or so, until the mixture starts to stick to the base of the pan. Remove from the heat and leave to stand for 1 minute before gradually adding the beaten eggs, stirring vigorously until you have a glossy dough with a dropping consistency. Spoon or pipe generous tablespoonfuls onto the prepared baking tray and bake for 25–30 minutes or until golden. Make a small hole in the side of each profiterole for the crème pâtissière, then cool on a wire rack.

To make the crème pâtissière, whisk the egg yolks with the sugar until light and fluffy, then stir in the flour. Place the milk and vanilla pod in a pan and bring to the boil. Remove the vanilla pod and turn the heat down to medium–low, then add the egg yolk mixture, whisking until the crème pâtissière returns to the boil and thickens. Pour into a bowl and cover with plastic wrap, pressing it onto the surface to stop a skin forming. Leave to cool before piping into the profiteroles.

Break the chocolate into a heatproof bowl and set over a pan of simmering water (don't let the bowl touch the water) to melt. In a separate pan, gently warm the cream. Pour the cream into the bowl of melted chocolate and whisk until you get a glossy, thick sauce.

Place the profiteroles on a serving plate, pour over the chocolate sauce and sprinkle with grated chocolate.

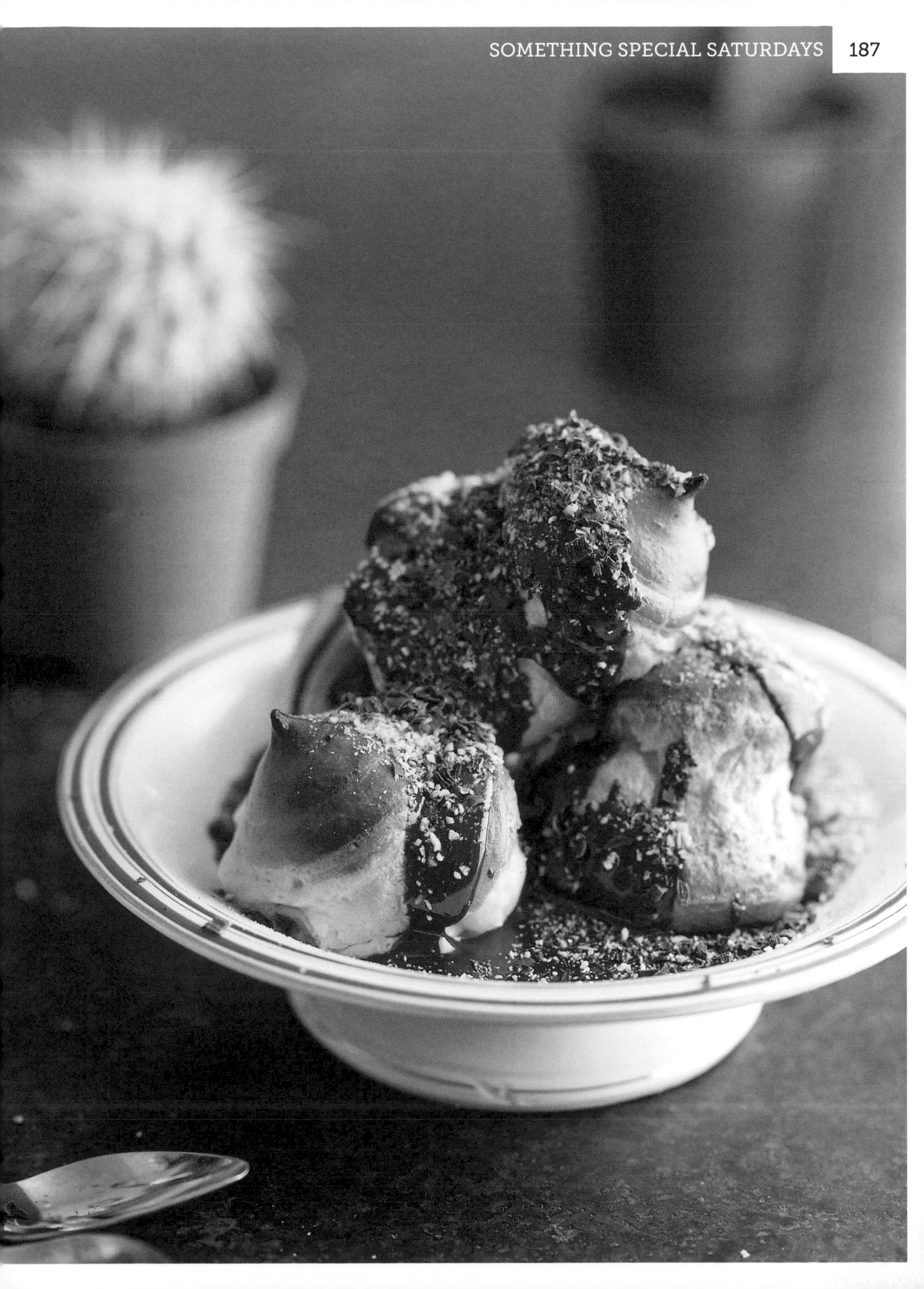

Preparation time: 20 minutes | **Cooking time:** 45 minutes | **Feeds:** 4–6

SPINACH & LEEK
SQUID INK PASTA BAKE

If you're in a hurry, you can flash the finished dish under a hot grill (broiler) for 5–10 minutes instead of baking it in the oven.

2–3 handfuls of left-over cooked squid ink pasta ribbons (see page 184) or 350–450 g (12 oz–1 lb) dried squid ink tagiatelle
glug of olive oil
500 g (1 lb 2 oz) spinach leaves, thoroughly rinsed
knob of butter
2 leeks, sliced
1 large white onion, diced
2 cloves garlic, thinly sliced

CHEESE SAUCE
50 g (1¾ oz) butter
1 tablespoon dijon mustard
2 heaped tablespoons plain (all-purpose) flour
600 ml (21 fl oz) milk
300 g (10½ oz/3 cups) grated mature cheddar
50 g (1¾ oz/½ cup) finely grated parmesan

Preheat the oven to 190°C (375°F/gas mark 5).

If using dried squid ink tagliatelle, cook it in a deep saucepan of boiling water with a glug of olive oil. Stir and, when the water has returned to the boil, cook for about 6–7 minutes or until al dente, then drain.

Using a fork, twist the pasta into small bundles and place in a baking dish

In a separate pan, cook the spinach over medium heat until it's wilted, then drain and spread evenly over the pasta in the baking dish. Melt the butter in a frying pan over medium heat, add the leeks, onion and garlic and cook for 5–6 minutes or until soft and starting to caramelise, then add to the baking dish as well.

For the cheese sauce, melt the butter in a saucepan over medium–low heat, then whisk in the mustard and flour until it forms a paste. Season with salt and pepper, then gradually add the milk, stirring constantly, until you have a thick smooth sauce. Add half of the grated cheddar and stir until it has melted into the sauce. Taste for additional seasoning and adjust if necessary.

Pour the cheese sauce into the baking dish, then sprinkle over the remaining cheddar and the parmesan. Bake for 20–25 minutes or until golden and crispy.

SLOW
SUNDAYS

Sunday is still the day of rest. There's no rushing about to be done, even if you're getting together for a family feast or brunch with friends. This section's got slow, satisfying cooking covered. You can opt for The Lazy Route or The Long Route. Just remember – don't hurry.

BREAKFAST
Horseradish Bloody Mary with Spicy Merguez Sausage Buttie
Nursing a hangover, or just in need of something hearty to kick-start the day?

LUNCH
Jerusalem Artichoke Soup with Crispy Sage & Shallots (v)
After that big start, lunch needs to be lighter.

SNACK
Pizza Style Puff Pastry Tart
Keeping it quick, but cooking for a crowd.

THELAZYROUTE

DINNER
Rustic Fish Stew of Cod Cheeks, Fennel, Mussels & Clams
You've raided the local fish shop and are up for cooking with bold flavours: this is a dinner for adults.

DESSERT
Lemon Zest, Elderflower & Rosemary Ice Pops (v)
Fancy something zingy and refreshing?

LEFTOVERS
Seafood Risotto

(v) = vegetarian option

Preparation time: 10 minutes | Cooking time: 10 minutes | Feeds: 4

HORSERADISH BLOODY MARY WITH SPICY MERGUEZ SAUSAGE BUTTIE

This, in all honesty, is for those mornings when you're feeling your worst, the night before has taken its toll, and you need something to blow the cobwebs away. My Uncle Nigel first introduced me to merguez sausages. He lived in the south of France, and he'd always cook them on the BBQ. If you're feeling too delicate to make your own merguez, cheat and get some from the butcher.

4 large crusty rolls
knob of butter
dijon mustard and hot ketchup
  (see opposite), to serve

HOMEMADE MERGUEZ

1½ teaspoons fennel seeds
2 teaspoons coriander seeds
500 g (1 lb 2 oz) good-quality minced
  (ground) lamb
2 cloves garlic, finely chopped
2 generous tablespoons harissa
½ teaspoon chilli flakes – optional

HORSERADISH BLOODY MARY

1 litre (35 fl oz/4 cups) good-quality
  tomato juice
4 double shots of good-quality vodka
dash of dry sherry
1 heaped teaspoon creamed
  horseradish
juice of ½ lemon
dash of Tabasco sauce
glug of worcestershire sauce
ice and your garnish of choice – celery
  stalks, rosemary sprigs, cornichons,
  olives, radishes, lemon or lime
  wedges, jalapeños

If you're going the whole hog here, make your own merguez sausages... using a pestle and mortar, grind the fennel and coriander seeds to a powder. Transfer to a bowl and add the lamb, garlic, harissa and a sprinkling of pepper. Add some chilli flakes if you want an extra kick, and mix thoroughly. Using your hands, take small handfuls and roll into rough burger or sausage shapes... or to fit your rolls.

Place a frying pan over high heat and, when it's hot, add the merguez and cook for 3–4 minutes on each side or until brown and crisp. (Alternatively, you could grill the sausages for 4–5 minutes on each side.)

For the horseradish bloody mary, combine all the ingredients in a large jug and stir well. Taste for seasoning and adjust with pepper, extra lemon juice, Tabasco and worcestershire sauce. Put ice into the glasses and pour over the bloody mary. I'm a fan of a big celery stalk, rosemary and a couple of cornichons chucked in too.

Spread the rolls with a thin layer of butter, followed by a thick coating of mustard and a generous dollop of hot ketchup. Add the merguez and serve immediately.

HOT KETCHUP

1 x 400 g (14 oz) jar of Peppadew hot
   whole sweet piquante peppers or
   chargrilled peppers (capsicums)
1 teaspoon soft brown sugar
3 sprigs of thyme, leaves only
sprinkling of chilli flakes

Use a hand blender to blitz all the ingredients
to a ketchup consistency – add a glug of oil
or liquid from the pepper jar if it's too thick.

Preparation time: 10 minutes | **Cooking time:** 35 minutes | **Feeds:** 4–6

JERUSALEM ARTICHOKE SOUP WITH CRISPY SAGE & SHALLOTS

This is a truly earthy, hearty dish. Until you've tried it for yourself, you won't get why it's so great.

1 kg (2 lb 4 oz) jerusalem artichokes, scrubbed clean
2 white onions, roughly chopped
2 glugs of rapeseed oil
1.5 litres (52 fl oz/6 cups) vegetable stock
2 shallots, thinly sliced
12 sage leaves
70 g (2½ oz/⅔ cup) finely grated parmesan
glug of extra virgin olive oil

Preheat the oven to 190°C (375°F/gas mark 5).

Cut the artichokes into 3 cm (1¼ in) cubes and place in a roasting tin with the onions. Season with salt and pepper and add a glug of rapeseed oil, then roast for 25 minutes. Add the vegetable stock to the roasting tin and cook for a further 10 minutes.

Meanwhile, pour a glug of rapeseed oil into a frying pan over medium heat and add the shallots and sage leaves, together with a pinch of salt. Fry for a few minutes until golden and crispy.

When the artichoke is cooked, remove from the oven and leave to cool for a minute or so before transferring the contents of the roasting tin to a blender and blitzing until smooth. Check the seasoning and adjust to your taste – I like lots of white and black pepper with this.

Pour the soup into bowls and garnish with a sprinkling of parmesan, the crispy shallots and sage leaves and a drizzle of extra virgin olive oil.

Preparation time: 10 minutes | **Cooking time:** 25 minutes | **Feeds:** 8–10

PIZZA STYLE PUFF PASTRY TART

We first made these on holiday one year in Puglia. Not wanting to miss a moment of sunlight, our time spent in the kitchen was brief. Ripe and fresh is what's crucial here. Keep the toppings simple and well seasoned and you'll be serving up a treat.

450 g (1 lb) pre-rolled puff pastry (about 2 rolls)
14–16 ripe cherry tomatoes
2 teaspoons dried oregano
2 small glugs of extra virgin olive oil, plus extra for drizzling
1 white onion, sliced into rings
250 g (9 oz) mozzarella, ideally buffalo, roughly torn
5 slices of prosciutto
2 large handfuls of basil leaves

Preheat the oven to 190°C (375°F/gas mark 5) and lightly oil two baking trays.

Lay the pre-rolled pastry on the baking sheets and cook in the oven for around 15 minutes or until golden brown, risen and cooked through.

Meanwhile, place the tomatoes, oregano and olive oil in a pan, season with salt and pepper, then cook over medium heat for around 10 minutes or until the tomatoes begin to soften. Add the onion and cook for 2 minutes – it should still be firm/crisp, but not entirely raw.

Top the cooked pastry with the mozzarella, followed by the tomatoes and onion, then return to the oven for a further 5–7 minutes until the cheese melts.

Drape over the prosciutto, then garnish with basil leaves, a drizzle of olive oil and black pepper.

TIP Leave out the prosciutto and add mushrooms for a vegetarian version.

Preparation time: 15 minutes | **Cooking time:** 30 minutes | **Feeds:** 6–8 (or 2–4 with leftovers)

RUSTIC FISH STEW OF COD CHEEKS, FENNEL, MUSSELS & CLAMS

If you're a seafood lover, then this one's for you. Go all out on the fish front. I try and buy whatever the fishmonger's recommending that day, which is how I discovered cod cheeks a few years back. Don't be afraid to try different things; if you let them know what you're making, they're usually pretty good at suggesting what's good and will work in your recipe. This is a great dish for when you need to cook for the masses.

glug of olive oil

2 white onions, roughly diced

1 fennel bulb, roughly diced – include any fronds

2 carrots, roughly diced

2 cloves garlic, finely chopped

1 red chilli, roughly chopped

1 teaspoon fennel seeds

3 teaspoons smoked paprika

glug of white wine

2 x 400 g (14 oz) tins of chopped tomatoes

3 bay leaves

1 litre (35 fl oz/4 cups) fish stock

500 g (1 lb 2 oz) mussels, scrubbed and debearded

300 g (10½ oz) clams, scrubbed and rinsed

350 g (12 oz) cod cheeks

handful of roughly chopped parsley

juice of 1 lime

Pour the oil into a large pan and place over medium heat. Add the onions, fennel and carrots and cook for 4–5 minutes, stirring occasionally. Add the garlic, chilli, fennel seeds and paprika, season with salt and pepper, and cook for another 4–5 minutes, stirring every now and then. Add the white wine, tomatoes, bay leaves and fish stock and simmer for 15 minutes, then have a taste and adjust the seasoning accordingly.

Add the mussels, clams and cod cheeks and increase the heat to high. Cover the pan with a lid (or foil) and cook for 2–4 minutes, giving the pan a shake after a couple of minutes. Once the mussels and clams have opened and the cod cheeks are cooked, remove the pan from the heat.

Sprinkle over the parsley, some extra black pepper and a squeeze of lime juice, then serve at least two big ladlefuls per person, making sure the fish and seafood is shared out equally.

A big crusty seeded loaf with butter is my favourite accompaniment to this. As is a nice glass of crisp white wine.

Preparation time: 5 minutes | **Freezing time:** 2–3 hours | **Feeds:** 6

LEMON ZEST, ELDERFLOWER & ROSEMARY ICE POPS

These are really refreshing and look beautiful. Perfect for the summer months.

1 litre (35 fl oz/4 cups) sparkling elderflower pressé or elderflower cordial mixed with soda water
juice of 1 lemon
finely grated zest of ½ lemon
6 sprigs of rosemary
1 x 6-mould ice-pop tray, plus sticks

Combine the elderflower pressé or diluted cordial with the lemon juice and zest, then pour into the moulds, adding a sprig of rosemary to each one. Place a stick in each ice pop and freeze for 2–3 hours.

TIP These are also great as ice cubes, dropped into a gin or vodka and tonic on a sunny evening.

Preparation time: 10 minutes | Cooking time: 30 minutes | Feeds: 4–6

SEAFOOD RISOTTO

This is a leftover dish that's not to be missed. In fact, there's no need to wait until you have the right leftovers to make this. After you've made it once, you'll realise just how simple it is... you'll be knocking this out every week.

650 ml (22½ fl oz) fish stock – combine with any juices from the left-over fish stew (see below)

50 g (1¾ oz) butter

2 shallots, diced

1 clove garlic, finely chopped

350 g (12 oz) arborio or other risotto rice

small glass of white wine

500–600 g (1 lb 2 oz–1 lb 5 oz) left-over seafood from rustic fish stew (see page 201) or a mixture of fresh mussels, clams, prawns and squid

small handful of finely chopped parsley

50 g (1¾ oz/½ cup) finely grated parmesan

drizzle of extra virgin olive oil

Start by heating three-quarters of the fish stock in a pan, then keep it warm.

Melt the butter in large heavy-based pan over medium–low heat and add the shallots and garlic. Season with salt and pepper and cook for a few minutes, then stir in the rice, coating every grain with the melted butter. Add the wine and bring to the boil, then immediately turn the temperature down to low. Gradually add the warm fish stock a little at a time, allowing the rice to absorb the liquid before adding any more and stirring the risotto constantly. The whole process should take around 10–15 minutes. The rice is done when it is al dente (still with a slight bite to it).

Pour the remaining stock into a pan and bring to the boil, then add the seafood. If you're using left-over seafood, gently heat it through for a few minutes. If you're cooking fresh seafood, cover the pan and cook for 2–4 minutes or until the mussels and clams have opened and the prawns and squid are just cooked.

When the seafood is done, transfer the stock from the pan to the risotto and stir for a minute or so, then add the seafood. Sprinkle in half the parsley and half the parmesan, then taste and adjust the seasoning as necessary.

Serve garnished with the remaining parsley and parmesan, plus a drizzle of extra virgin olive oil.

TIP To be on the safe side, don't keep left-over fish and seafood for longer than two days. And make sure it stays in the fridge until you're ready to use it.

BREAKFAST
Spanish Style Start to the Day (v)
You have all time in the world, why rush?

LUNCH
Braised Steak Chilli Con Carne with Tangy Orange Slaw
You're organised and have planned ahead.

SNACK
Patatas Bravas with Crispy Fried Halloumi (v)
Can't resist roasting potatoes on a Sunday?

THE**LONG**ROUTE

DINNER
Asian BBQ Pulled Pork
Not sticking to the traditional Sunday roast?

DESSERT
Sticky Toffee Crème Brûlées (v)
Up for going all out?

LEFTOVERS
Spinach, Sage & Ricotta Crispy Fried Gnudi
with Pork Ragu

(v) = vegetarian option

Preparation time: 10 minutes | **Cooking time:** 50 minutes | **Feeds:** 4–6

SPANISH STYLE
START TO THE DAY

If you're partial to going big on breakfast, this is the dish for you. The padrón peppers, hollandaise sauce, crisp and cheesy roasted potatoes and fried egg are always on the breakfast wish list. This takes some co-ordinating, but if you're prepared and keen to create a feast, then get stuck in.

5 large maris piper or desiree potatoes
few glugs of rapeseed oil
few knobs of butter
12 cherry tomatoes
100 g (3½ oz/1 cup) grated mature
   cheddar
300 g (10½ oz) spinach leaves,
   thoroughly washed
1 white onion, thinly sliced
300 g (10½ oz) padrón peppers
4–6 eggs – one per person
small handful of coriander
   (cilantro) leaves
1 spring onion (scallion), thinly sliced
1 red chilli, thinly sliced

HOLLANDAISE SAUCE
125 g (4½ oz) butter
1 tablespoon white wine vinegar
2 large egg yolks – or 3 medium ones
juice of ½ lemon

Scrub the potatoes, but leave the skin on, then cut into 2 cm (¾ in) cubes. Add to boiling salted water and cook for 12–15 minutes or until tender. Drain and put in a shallow roasting tin. Add a few glugs of oil, along with a couple of knobs of butter, and toss to coat the potatoes. Season with salt and pepper, then add the cherry tomatoes and half of the cheese. Place under the grill (broiler) for 8–10 minutes or until the cheese starts to crisp and bubble. Keep an eye on it, and once one side has a nice crunchy texture, turn the potatoes, adding the rest of the cheese. Return to the grill for another 8–10 minutes until you have golden, cheesy potatoes.

Meanwhile, cook the spinach in a frying pan over medium heat until it wilts, then remove from the pan and set aside. Add a small glug of oil, the onion, padrón peppers and a good pinch of salt, then cook over high heat for 3–4 minutes or until the onion and peppers have softened. Remove from the pan and keep warm. Add a little more oil to the pan and fry an egg per person.

For the hollandaise sauce, warm the butter and vinegar in a small saucepan over medium–low heat. When it is just warm, gradually add to your egg yolks and whisk until thick, smooth and creamy. Season with salt and pepper before adding the lemon juice. Give the sauce another thorough whisk, then serve immediately.

I like to serve this up as a sharing dish on a board or plate. Start with the potatoes and tomatoes before piling on the spinach, onions and padrón peppers, followed by the coriander and then your fried eggs. Finish with the sliced spring onion and chilli.

Preparation time: 20 minutes | **Cooking time:** 4–5 hours | **Feeds:** 4–6

BRAISED STEAK CHILLI CON CARNE
WITH TANGY ORANGE SLAW

This is perfect for days when you need something that can be left to cook.

1.5 kg (3 lb 5 oz) braising steak
2 tablespoons plain (all-purpose) flour
glug of rapeseed oil
2 red onions, diced
1 large carrot, diced
1 celery stalk, diced
4 cloves garlic, chopped
6 cm (2½ in) knob of ginger, chopped
1 tablespoon dried oregano
2 teaspoons ground cumin
1 tablespoon fennel seeds
½–1 teaspoon chilli powder, to taste
1 heaped tablespoon smoked paprika
½ teaspoon ground cinnamon
1 tablespoon cocoa powder
875 ml (30 fl oz/3½ cups) beef stock
1 x 400 g (14 oz) tin of tomatoes
2 x 400 g (14 oz) tins of kidney beans,
   drained and rinsed
handful of chopped coriander (cilantro)
3 radishes, thinly sliced
1 red chilli, thinly sliced
2 limes, cut into quarters
pita bread or pita shovels, to serve

TANGY ORANGE SLAW
1 medium-sized red cabbage, shredded
1 large orange, peeled and sliced
handful of chopped coriander (cilantro)
glug of red wine vinegar
3 tablespoons crème fraîche
   (sour cream)

Preheat the oven to 160°C (315°F/gas mark 2–3).

Cut the braising steak into three pieces. Put the flour in a shallow bowl and season with salt and pepper, then dust the braising steak in the flour. Pour a glug of oil into a flameproof casserole dish over medium–high heat and brown the steak on all sides, then remove and set aside. Next add the onions, carrot, celery, garlic and ginger and cook for a few minutes over medium–low heat until they soften. Return the steak to the dish, then add the oregano and spices and cook for a few minutes. Stir in the cocoa powder, stock, tomatoes and kidney beans. Make sure the steak is covered with liquid – add a dash of water, if necessary, then cover with a lid or foil and braise in the oven for 4–5 hours or until the meat is fall-apart tender. Have a look after 3 hours and give it all a stir; if there's still a lot of liquid, remove the lid for the last hour or so. When it's ready, shred the steak with two forks, so you get delicious long strands of beef. Garnish the chilli with chopped coriander, slices of radish and chilli, and lime quarters.

For the slaw, combine the cabbage, orange (including any juice) and coriander in a bowl. Mix the red wine vinegar and creme fraiche with salt and white pepper to taste, then add to the bowl and toss thoroughly.

Serve this up buffet style, so people can help themselves, using the pita shovels to scoop up as much slaw and chilli as possible.

TIP To make pita shovels to go with your chilli con carne, drizzle pita bread with olive oil, sprinkle with smoked paprika and bake for 5 minutes or until golden.

Preparation time: 10 minutes | **Cooking time:** 30 minutes | **Feeds:** 4–6

PATATAS BRAVAS WITH CRISPY FRIED HALLOUMI

Who doesn't love a roast potato with a warm smoky sauce? I love this just as is or with a crisp green salad. This is a vegetarian favourite in my household.

1 kg (2 lb 4 oz) new potatoes,
   cut in half
4 cloves garlic
generous glug of rapeseed oil
sprinkle of smoked paprika
250 g (9 oz) halloumi, cut into
   5 mm (¼ in) slices and then
   each slice cut in half
small handful of chopped parsley
½ spring onion (scallion), thinly sliced
1 teaspoon finely grated lemon zest

TOMATO SAUCE
glug of rapeseed oil
½ red onion, sliced
3 cloves garlic, finely chopped
1 heaped teaspoon smoked paprika
½ teaspoon chilli flakes
1 x 400 g (14 oz) tin of tomatoes
dash of Tabasco sauce
dash of red wine vinegar
2 sprigs of rosemary

Preheat the oven to 190°C (375°F/gas mark 5).

Put the potatoes and whole garlic cloves in a roasting tin. Drizzle with oil, season with salt and sprinkle over the smoked paprika, then roast for 20–25 minutes or until golden and crispy.

Meanwhile, make your tomato sauce. Pour a glug of oil into a pan over medium heat and add the onion, garlic, smoked paprika and chilli flakes. Season with salt and pepper and cook for a minute or two until the onion has softened, then add the tomatoes, Tabasco, vinegar and rosemary. Stir well, then taste. You're aiming for a balance of sweet, smoky and spicy – add more chilli flakes or paprika for more kick.

Add the roast potatoes and garlic to the sauce, coating them thoroughly, then turn the heat down to low.

Heat a non-stick frying pan over medium–high heat, then add the halloumi and sear for 1–2 minutes or until the cheese is golden and crispy. I prefer not to fry both sides so you get half soft, half crispy cheese, but it's up to you.

Combine the halloumi with the potatoes in tomato sauce and garnish with the parsley, spring onion and lemon zest. Get stuck in!

STICKY BBQ SAUCE
2 tablespoons basting syrup (see opposite)
2 whole star anise
½ teaspoon five-spice powder
250 ml (9 fl oz/1 cup) chicken stock
50 g (1¾ oz) caster (superfine) sugar
½ red chilli, seeds removed, finely diced
1 teaspoon white pepper
2 tablespoons light soy sauce
2 teaspoons dark soy sauce
small shaving of orange zest
2 teaspoons cornflour (cornstarch)

Put all the ingredients except the cornflour
in a pan and cook over medium heat for
15–20 minutes until reduced and sticky. Mix
the cornflour to a paste with a dash of cold
water, then stir into the sauce and simmer
to thicken. Taste to check you have the right
balance of sweet, fragrant and peppery.

Preparation time: 20 minutes | **Marinating time:** overnight | **Cooking time:** up to 7 hours | **Feeds:** 4–6 (or 2 with leftovers)

ASIAN BBQ PULLED PORK

If you want your BBQ pork to have the distinctive red colour of the pork you get in Chinatown, add a couple of teaspoons of red food colouring to the marinade, syrup and sauce. It'll taste just as good without it, though. Serve with egg fried rice or plain old jasmine rice and some stir-fried greens.

1.5 kg (3 lb 5 oz) pork belly,
   in one piece
lime halves, chopped coriander
   (cilantro), red chilli slices, toasted
   black sesame seeds and sticky BBQ
   sauce (see opposite), to serve

MARINADE

5 spring onions (scallions), chopped
handful of coriander (cilantro) roots,
   chopped
3 red Asian shallots, finely chopped
big chunk of ginger (about 15 cm/
   6 in), bruised and roughly chopped
big chunk of galangal (about 12 cm/
   4½ in), bruised and roughly chopped
2 whole star anise
3 cloves
2 teaspoons five-spice powder
2 tablespoons dark soy sauce
3 tablespoons Chinese rice wine
150 g (5½ oz) caster (superfine) sugar

BASTING SYRUP

5 tablespoons caster (superfine) sugar
1 tablespoon light soy sauce
2 tablespoons hoisin sauce
1 tablespoon honey

Put all the marinade ingredients in a large casserole dish with 1.5 litres (6 cups) of water and bring to the boil. Simmer for 10–15 minutes, then leave to cool completely. Add the pork and marinate overnight in the fridge.

The next day, preheat the oven 250°C (500°F/gas mark 9) and make the basting syrup by combining all the ingredients.

Remove the pork from its marinade and pat dry. Place in a roasting tin and roast for 25 minutes or until the fat starts to blister. Turn the oven down to 160°C (315°F/gas mark 2–3) and cook for at least 3 hours, or up to 7 hours. Turn the meat every 2–3 hours and, during the last hour, turn and baste the pork every 10–15 minutes. When it's ready, the skin should be crispy; if it's not, blast it under a hot grill for a few minutes before serving.

Shred the pork and serve with lime, coriander, chilli and sesame seeds. Drizzle a little sticky BBQ sauce over the meat, then pour the remaining sauce into a jug so people can help themselves.

TIP If you can't find galangal, just double up on the ginger.

Preparation time: 25 minutes | **Cooking time:** 1 hour 40 minutes | **Feeds:** 6 (with leftovers)

STICKY TOFFEE CRÈME BRÛLÉES

This dessert is a combination of my two all-time favourites. What's great about this recipe is that you can make it well in advance if you're having friends round – and it makes plenty of sticky toffee pudding, so there's always loads left over to get you through the next week!

STICKY TOFFEE PUDDING
100 g (3½ oz) dark muscovado (brown) sugar
165 g (5¾ oz) self-raising (self-rising) flour
125 ml (4 fl oz/½ cup) whole milk
1 large egg
1 teaspoon vanilla extract
50 g (1¾ oz) unsalted butter, melted
300 g (10½ oz) dates, roughly chopped

STICKY TOFFEE SAUCE
200 g (7 oz) dark muscovado (brown) sugar
25 g (1 oz) unsalted butter, cut into small cubes
500 ml (17 fl oz/2 cups) boiling water

CRÈME BRÛLÉE
900 ml (32 fl oz) double (thick) cream
1 vanilla pod (bean), split and seeds scraped
9 egg yolks
45 g (1¾ oz) caster (superfine) sugar
3 tablespoons demerara (brown) sugar

Preheat the oven to 190°C (375°F/gas mark 5).

In a bowl, combine all the sticky toffee sponge ingredients, then pour into a deep greased or non-stick rectangular baking tin (about 30 x 20 cm/12 x 8 in). For the sticky toffee sauce, scatter the sugar over the sponge mixture, along with the cubes of butter, then pour over the boiling water. Cook in the oven for around 40–50 minutes. You'll be left with a gooey, sweet and sticky toffee pudding. Let this cool and it's ready to use as the surprise centre of your crème brûlée.

Reduce the oven temperature to 150°C (300°F/gas mark 2) and place six small ramekins in a roasting tin.

For the crème brûlée, pour the cream into a small, heavy-based pan and add the vanilla pod and seeds. Bring to the boil over a medium–low heat – as soon as it starts to bubble, take it off the heat and remove the vanilla pod. In a heatproof bowl or jug, mix the egg yolks and caster sugar until just combined then pour in the cream, stirring well to mix.

Divide the sticky toffee pudding between the ramekins: aim for a generous teaspoonful, along with a bit of the sauce, then pour in the cream and egg yolk mixture until it completely covers the sticky toffee pudding. Place the ramekins in a roasting tin or baking dish tin, then pour in enough cold water to come two-thirds of the way up the sides of the ramekins. Bake for about 40 minutes until the custard has set – it should only wobble a little when given a gentle shake. Allow to cool, then chill until ready to eat.

Before serving, sprinkle the tops of the cold crème brûlées with demerara sugar and caramelise the tops with a kitchen blowtorch or under a hot grill (broiler).

Preparation time: 10 minutes | **Cooking time:** 1½ hours | **Feeds:** 4

SPINACH, SAGE & RICOTTA CRISPY FRIED GNUDI WITH PORK RAGU

This dish is delicious all on its own, even without the left-over pork, so you can choose whether to serve this up as a vegetarian delight or smother it in rich pork ragu. Gnudi is like a lighter version of gnocchi – you can think of it as naked ravioli, with all the tasty filling but minus the pasta.

GNUDI

225 g (8 oz/1 cup) ricotta
100 g (3½ oz/1 cup) finely grated
   parmesan
150 g (5½ oz/1 cup) plain (all-purpose)
   flour or '00' flour
200 g (7 oz) frozen spinach, thawed
   and squeezed dry
4 egg yolks, lightly beaten
½ nutmeg, finely grated
finely grated zest of ½ lemon
1 tablespoon finely chopped parsley
bunch of sage leaves, half finely
   chopped, half left whole
knob of butter
glug of olive oil
140 g (5 oz/1 cup) frozen peas

PORK RAGU

handful of left-over pulled pork
   (see page 215), shredded
glug of olive oil
½ red onion, finely diced
2 cloves garlic, thinly sliced
1 x 400 g (14 oz) tin of tomatoes
glug of red wine
1 teaspoon sugar

For the pork ragu, allow the left-over pork to come to room temperature. Pour a glug of oil into a pan over medium heat and add the onion and garlic, then cook for a few minutes until the onion softens. Add the tomatoes, red wine and sugar, and season with salt and pepper. Cook over medium–low heat for an hour or so, then add the pork 10 minutes prior to serving, just to heat through.

Bring a large pan of salted water to the boil while you prepare the gnudi. Combine the ricotta, parmesan and flour in a bowl. Add the spinach, egg yolks, nutmeg, lemon zest, parsley and the chopped sage, then season with salt and pepper. Use a fork to mix thoroughly. Roll generous teaspoonfuls of the mixture into balls.

When the water is boiling, add 6–7 balls at a time and cook for a minute or so, just until they float to the surface, then remove. Repeat until all the gnudi are cooked.

In a large frying pan, melt a small knob of butter with a glug of oil over high heat, then add the cooked gnudi and the whole sage leaves. Fry until the gnudi are crispy and golden, turning them every few minutes. Add the peas and the pork ragu and cook for a few minutes longer, just to heat through.

TIP Any left-over pork ragu is great served with pasta; if you can't face pork two days on the trot, freeze it for later.

THANKS...

... to Trev, my vegetarian veg-spiration: the most patient, kind and inventive man I know. You're the best; definitely couldn't have got this together without you.

... to Krispy, I owe you 100 hours – you're amazing. Thank you for all the help getting the book pitch together in the first place (that was pretty much a book in itself).

... to Lew, for making all the bits between the recipes make sense so I can sound like a pro!

... to my dad, for all those roast dinners, and for teaching me how to really pack down a good meal and love every bite.

... to Nan, who at 85 still makes the best desserts around, writes the recipes out by hand and posts them to me. Every cake, every shepherd's pie, every mince pie (of which I've consumed hundreds) has made me want to cook, mainly so that I can relive those mouthfuls.

... to Grandad, for his precision vegetable-cutting and providing so much humour at the dinner table – and for typewriting out his jokes and sending them to me. You're the funniest man I know.

... to my mum, who encouraged us to cook and try all sorts of cuisines that I now couldn't live without, and for sous-chefing the pop-ups.

... to my bro, who's just there to test how much I really can eat and push me to my limits (I'll never shy away from those challenges).

... to Ted the dog, who rarely turns his nose up at whatever I put down for him, and who keeps me company for hours while I cook.

... and to my housemates and mates, for always being willing eaters, and to everyone who has tested all the recipes over the years and specifically for this book. Having people to cook for makes it all worthwhile. No one likes to eat alone.

Extra big thanks to Murdoch Books, for giving me the chance to make a book (I couldn't be more excited). To photographer Alan Benson, to food stylist Iain Graham and home economist Wilson Chung – I had so much fun and food while making this. I can't thank you enough. To editor and designer, Alison Cowan and Tania Gomes, thanks for turning this into a proper book. To George Chevalier Lewis for his photographs; and to Hellie Ogden at Janklow & Nesbit for making this all happen in the first place.

Other people I would like to thank for all their help along the way – Bernie, Cal, Cropper, Krispy, George, Apphia, God-daughter Tallis, Katie Dent, Angela Wells, Lizzee Crees, Waggy, Gills, Grim, Kel, Hens, Jess, Carol, Weir, Deano, Cara, Andy Jones, Tom Gormer, Lew, Hels, Bons, Dan, Mikey, Ry, El. All the sisters, Shell, Hayle, Kate, Sam (plus the brother-in-laws) and, of course, my second mum, Jill.

INDEX

Published in 2015 by Murdoch Books, an imprint of Allen & Unwin

Murdoch Books Australia
83 Alexander Street
Crows Nest NSW 2065
Phone: +61 (0)2 8425 0100
Fax: +61 (0)2 9906 2218
murdochbooks.com.au
info@murdochbooks.com.au

Murdoch Books UK
Erico House, 6th Floor
93–99 Upper Richmond Road
Putney, London SW15 2TG
Phone: +44 (0) 20 8785 5995
murdochbooks.co.uk
info@murdochbooks.co.uk

For Corporate Orders & Custom Publishing contact Noel Hammond,
National Business Development Manager, Murdoch Books Australia

Publisher: Corinne Roberts
Editorial Manager: Jane Price
Design Manager: Vivien Valk
Photographer: Alan Benson
Styling & Food Preparation: Iain Graham & Wilson Chung
Editor: Alison Cowan
Designer: Tania Gomes
Production Manager: Mary Bjelobrk

Text © Anna Barnett 2015
Design © Murdoch Books 2015
Photography © Alan Benson 2015

A cataloguing-in-publication entry is available from the catalogue of
the National Library of Australia at nla.gov.au.

ISBN 978 1 7433 6541 0 Australia
ISBN 978 1 7433 6542 7 UK

A catalogue record for this book is available from the British Library.

Colour reproduction by Splitting Image Colour Studio Pty Ltd,
Clayton, Victoria, Australia
Printed by C&C Offset Printing Co Ltd, China

IMPORTANT: Those who might be at risk from the effects of
salmonella poisoning (the elderly, pregnant women, young children
and those suffering from immune deficiency diseases) should consult
their doctor with any concerns about eating raw eggs.

OVEN GUIDE: You may find that cooking times vary, depending on
the oven you are using. For fan-forced ovens, as a general rule, set the
oven temperature to 20°C (35°F) lower than indicated in the recipe.